MARVEL

ULTIMATE FACT BOOK

ARE YOU A MARVEL EXPERT?

WRITTEN BY
MELANIE SCOTT

CONTENTS

Super Heroes

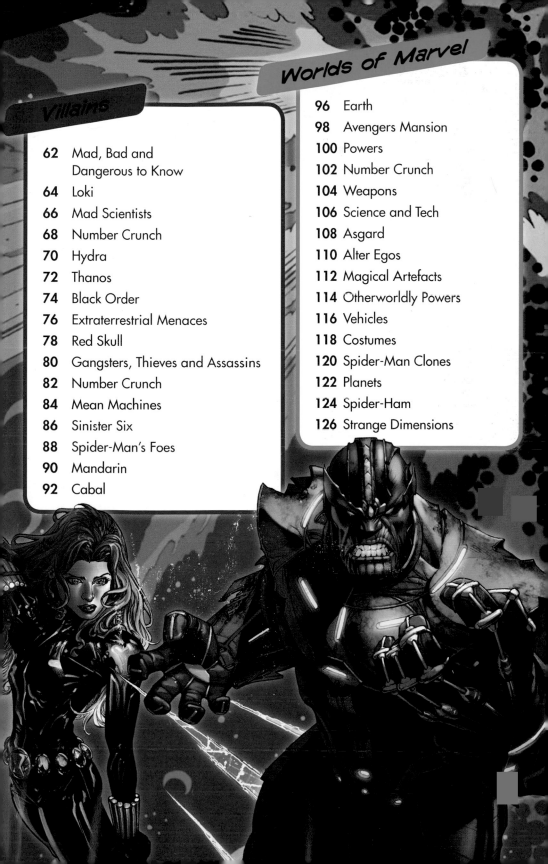

Villains

Worlds of Marvel

Captain Marvel

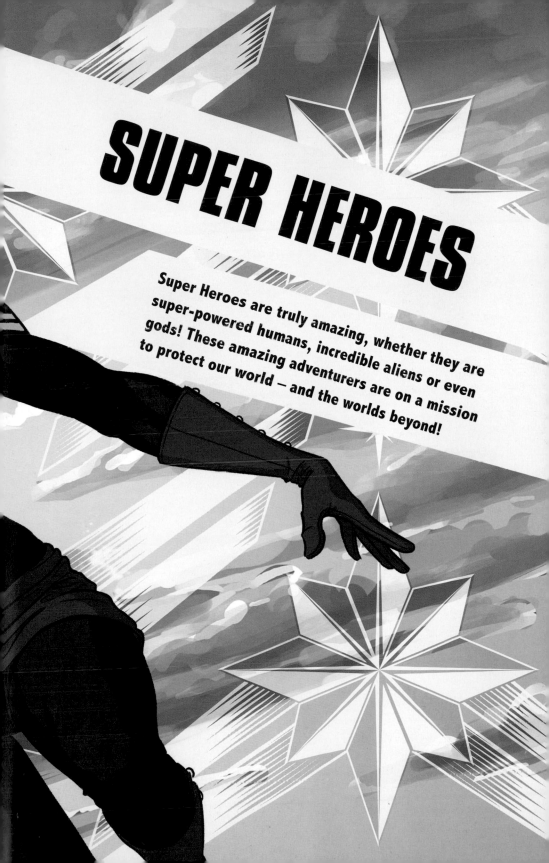

SUPER HEROES

Super Heroes are truly amazing, whether they are super-powered humans, incredible aliens or even gods! These amazing adventurers are on a mission to protect our world — and the worlds beyond!

CAPTAIN AMERICA

A war hero turned Super Hero, Captain America is one of Earth's greatest defenders. How much do you know about this powerful patriot?

1 Who took Captain America's place when Cap's serum wore off and he aged rapidly?
a. Sam Wilson
b. Thor
c. Sam Alexander
d. Hank Pym

2 In which year was Captain America born?
a. 1905
b. 1918
c. 1922
d. 1940

3 Which of these is NOT one of Cap's super-powers?
a. Slow ageing
b. Super-strength
c. Super-speed
d. Telepathy

4 What serum gave Captain America his powers?
a. Super-Rebirth
b. Super-Strength
c. Awesome-America
d. Super-Soldier

5 What super-team is Cap part of?
a. Fantastic Four
b. Avengers
c. Defenders
d. Alpha Flight

6 When he was rejected from the army, what classification was he given?
a. N-0
b. 4-F
c. X-2
d. 2-C

7

What is Cap's shield made from?
a. Omnium
b. Adamantium
c. Vibranium
d. Prometheum

8

In the Mangaverse alternate universe, which female character took on the role of Captain America?
a. Jocasta
b. Carol Danvers
c. Sharon Carter
d. Julia Carpenter

Genius Question

For a brief period, Captain America changed his name when he became disillusioned with politics. What did he change it to?

9

Which city does Captain America call home?
a. Los Angeles
b. Chicago
c. New York City
d. Boston

10

Who rescued Cap when he was frozen in a block of ice?
a. The Avengers
b. Black Panther
c. Black Widow
d. Guardians of the Galaxy

11

Who once broke Cap's shield with an Infinity Gauntlet?
a. Kang
b. Thanos
c. Baron Zemo
d. Hydra

13

What is Captain America's real name?
a. Matthew Murdock
b. Roger Stevenson
c. Norman Osborn
d. Steve Rogers

12

Which doctor once tried to make Cap go insane?
a. Doctor Doom
b. Doctor Voodoo
c. Doctor Faustus
d. Doctor Octopus

15

Who is Cap's oldest friend?
a. Nick Fury
b. Bucky Barnes
c. Baron Zemo
d. Tony Stark

14

Who is Cap's greatest foe?
a. Purple Man
b. Red Skull
c. Green Goblin
d. Scarlet Witch

16

Captain America was once turned into which beast?
a. Spider
b. Werewolf
c. Serpent
d. Sabre-toothed tiger

6 THINGS YOU NEED TO KNOW ABOUT...

Captain Marvel

1 Carol Danvers, a.k.a. Captain Marvel, used to be a pilot in the U.S. Air Force, before joining the space agency N.A.S.A.

2 Carol has incredible superpowers, which she gets through her half-Kree DNA. She has super-strength, and can fly and fire energy blasts.

3 Captain Marvel has belonged to several super-teams, including the Avengers, Guardians of the Galaxy, Ultimates and Alpha Flight.

4 Carol Danvers has also used the Super Hero code names Ms Marvel, Warbird and Binary.

5 During her time in the U.S.A.F., Carol carries out covert ops. As well as her spy skills, she speaks multiple languages, including the alien tongues of the Kree and Shi'ar.

6 As a pilot, Carol's nickname, or call sign, was Cheeseburger, following an unfortunate bout of sickness during G-Force training!

IRON MAN

Billionaire genius Tony Stark creates a suit of armour that transforms him into the invincible Iron Man. How much do you know about the Golden Avenger?

Which damaged body part is Tony Stark's first Iron Man ARMOUR built to protect?

a. Brain   c. Eyes

b. Heart   d. Toenails

Iron Man builds a special super-strong armour designed to take down which of his fellow AVENGERS?

a. Thor   c. Hulk

b. Hawkeye   d. War Machine

TRUE OR FALSE?

Tony Stark has no siblings.

4 What is the name of Tony Stark's BUTLER?

a. Davis   c. Jervis

b. Jarvis   d. Captain America

Which of these did Hawkeye come up with as a NICKNAME for Iron Man?

a. Shell-Head   c. Goldilocks

b. Web-Head   d. Glamour Pants

6 What was the name of the TEENAGER who replaced Tony Stark while he was in a coma?

a. Kiki Williams

b. Riri Stark

c. Virginia Stark

d. Riri Williams

7 And what was her CODENAME?

a. Iron Girl   c. Ironheart

b. Ironface   d. Grid Iron

10 TRUE OR FALSE?
Iron Man owns suspected alien investigation site Area 51.

11 Which of these teams has Iron Man never been a **MEMBER** of?
a. X-Men
b. Guardians of the Galaxy
c. West Coast Avengers
d. S.H.I.E.L.D.

12 What is the name for the **TECH** in Iron Man's armour that enables him to fly and fire energy beams?
a. Propulsor   c. Ascensor
b. Repulsor   d. Zoom

Genius Question
What is the name of the evil Russian version of Iron Man?

13 Who was the eminent physics **PROFESSOR** who helped Tony Stark build the first Iron Man armour?
a. Bo Minsen   c. Ho Yinsen
b. Mo Binsen   d. Yo Hinsen

8 Which of these is not a close **FRIEND** of Tony Stark?
a. Happy Hogan
b. Pepper Potts
c. James Rhodes
d. Justin Hammer

14 TRUE OR FALSE?
Tony Stark was held captive when he built the first Iron Man suit.

9 What is the name of Iron Man's adoptive **FATHER**?
a. Howard Stark
b. Mark Stark
c. Steve Rogers
d. Jason Stark

15 Where was Iron Man's Stark **TOWER** headquarters?
a. New York City
b. Los Angeles
c. Washington, D.C.
d. Chicago

ANSWERS

1b **2**c **3** False – Although he didn't know it when he was growing up, Tony has an adoptive brother, Arno. **4**b **5**a **6**d **7**c **8**d **9**a **10** True – Stark bought the abandoned U.S.A.F. base to store one of the Infinity Stones. **11**a **12**b **13**c **14** True – He had been captured by terrorists while demonstrating Stark military tech. **15**a **Genius Question** Crimson Dynamo

TEAM-UP

The Avengers

The Avengers are known as Earth's Mightiest Heroes, and it's not hard to see why! Meet the powerful heroes who are members of the ultimate super-team.

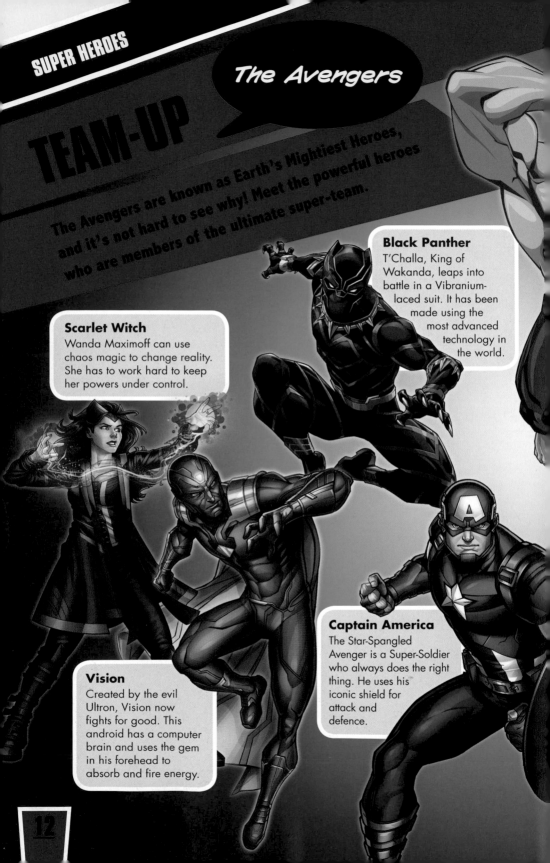

Black Panther

T'Challa, King of Wakanda, leaps into battle in a Vibranium-laced suit. It has been made using the most advanced technology in the world.

Scarlet Witch

Wanda Maximoff can use chaos magic to change reality. She has to work hard to keep her powers under control.

Captain America

The Star-Spangled Avenger is a Super-Soldier who always does the right thing. He uses his iconic shield for attack and defence.

Vision

Created by the evil Ultron, Vision now fights for good. This android has a computer brain and uses the gem in his forehead to absorb and fire energy.

Thor
The mighty Asgardian protects "Midgard" with his magical war hammer, Mjolnir. The god of thunder is arguably the strongest Avenger.

Wasp
The size-changing Wasp can fly and "sting" with powerful bioelectric blasts. She has been a leader of the Avengers team.

Hulk
Sometimes described as a monster, the gamma-spawned Hulk is extremely strong. His alter ego, Bruce Banner, is incredibly clever.

Falcon
Sam Wilson has a harness that allows him to fly. He also has a telepathic link to birds, including his falcon sidekick, Redwing.

Iron Man
The man in the iron suit is inventive genius Tony Stark. He is one of the key members of the Avengers.

Hawkeye
One of the few Avengers with no super-powers, Clint Barton's awesome archery skills help him hold his own alongside his enhanced teammates.

Black Widow
Former super spy Natasha Romanoff is a master martial artist. She was injected with a serum as a child that gave her enhanced strength, speed and healing abilities.

SPIDER-MAN

Peter Parker is the amazing Spider-Man, a wall-crawling, web-slinging hero who uses his strength and courage to protect his friendly neighbourhood... and beyond.

True or False?

1 Peter Parker is from Queens, New York City.

2 Peter Parker is born with his Super Hero powers.

3 Peter Parker is a janitor at the *Daily Bugle* newspaper.

4 Spider-Man's abilities include wall-climbing, web-shooting and super-strength.

5 The first villain Spider-Man faced was Green Goblin.

6 Spider-Man has a tingling spider-sense to warn him of danger.

7 Peter Parker's best friend later becomes his enemy, the Green Goblin.

8 The Ultimate Spider-Man from Earth-1610 is Ben Reilly.

9 Spider-Man's enemy Venom became the Superior Spider-Man.

10 As an adult, Peter Parker owned a multibillion-dollar corporation.

11 Peter Parker's middle name is Benjamin.

12 At one point Spider-Man wears a black costume from outer space.

13 Peter Parker's favourite class in school is English.

14 Peter Parker is a fan of the Boston Red Sox baseball team.

15 Tony Stark, a.k.a. Iron Man, creates special armour for Spider-Man.

16 Peter Parker's parents were called Ben and May Parker.

17 Peter Parker attended Midtown High School.

18 Spider-Man is good friends with Johnny Storm, a.k.a. the Human Torch.

19 Aunt May makes Spider-Man's first costume.

20 Before becoming a hero, Peter Parker tries to make it as a wrestler.

21 Spider-Man once revealed his true identity on live TV.

22 Mary Jane Watson is Peter Parker's next-door neighbour.

ANSWERS

1 True – It is his friendly neighbourhood!
2 False – He is bitten by a radioactive spider.
3 False – He was a photographer.
4 True – Wall-climbing and super-strength are super-powers, but Spidey builds his web shooters himself.
5 False – He faced villains like Chameleon and Electro before the Green Goblin.
6 True – He is always ready for the bad guys!

7 True – Harry Osborn takes over the Goblin identity from his father, Norman.
8 False – Miles Morales is the Ultimate Spider-Man.
9 False – It was Doctor Octopus, who thought he could do a better job than Spidey!
10 True – It was called Parker Industries.
11 True – His middle name honours his Uncle Ben.

12 True – After Spidey gets rid of the costume it merges with Eddie Brock to become the villainous Venom.
13 False – It is science, which he happens to be very good at.
14 False – He is a New York Mets fan.
15 True – It is nicknamed the Iron Spider.
16 False – They were Richard and Mary Parker.
17 True – He even fought Super Villains in the halls!

18 True – The two bond over their shared experiences as young heroes.
19 False – Peter makes it himself.
20 True – But he soon realises that the right thing to do is to use his powers to help people.
21 True – However, a magic spell cast by Doctor Strange caused everyone to forget what they had seen.
22 True – She too lives with an aunt in Queens.

TEAM-UP

Spider-Verse

Spider-Man is not the only spider-powered hero. In fact, there are several others on Earth and many more throughout the Multiverse!

Spider-Girl
After fighting alongside Jessica Drew, Anya Corazon joins the Warriors of the Great Web to protect other heroes across the Multiverse.

Spider-Gwen
Earth-65's Gwen Stacy becomes Spider-Woman. Gwen fights crime while also trying to maintain a normal life.

Ben Reilly
Ben is a clone of Peter Parker. For a time, he believes himself to be the real Spider-Man, but Ben later becomes the hero Scarlet Spider.

Spider-Woman
Jessica Drew gains her spider powers as a child. Tricked into becoming a Hydra agent, she later fights with the Avengers and S.H.I.E.L.D.

Ultimate Spider-Man
Earth-1610's Miles Morales ends up in the original Spider-Man's reality. Quickly settling in, he joins the Avengers and later the Champions.

Spider-Ham
Peter Porker is the spider hero of Earth-8311, a world of talking animals. Born a spider, he becomes a pig with spider powers after being bitten by a pig.

Spider-Man 2099
Miguel O'Hara is a science genius from the year 2099 who has given himself spider powers. He later travels in time to meet the original Spider-Man.

Kaine
This clone of Peter Parker is an enemy of Spider-Man before redeeming himself and becoming a hero. Like Ben Reilly, Kaine becomes Scarlet Spider.

Silk
Cindy Moon is bitten by the same spider that bites Peter Parker. Kept locked up for her own safety, she escapes and becomes the hero Silk.

Spider-UK
Billy Braddock is the Spider-Man of Earth-833. He is chosen as a protector of spider heroes and their worlds throughout the Multiverse.

The first user of the Ant-Man identity is Hank Pym. He creates "Pym Particles" that enable him to change size.

1

We really did something *GOOD* here.
Hank Pym

Ant-Man is now Scott Lang, a former thief. He steals Pym's Ant-Man suit in a desperate attempt to help his sick daughter, Cassie.

2

As well as changing size, Ant-Man can communicate with and control ants. He uses them to travel around on, and uses winged ants to fly.

3

Scott Lang is an electronics expert and is able to further his studies while in prison for burglary.

4

Ant-Man's powers come entirely from his suit. His helmet enables him to change size and "talk" to ants.

5

Lang has been a member of the Guardians of the Galaxy, Heroes for Hire and the Nova Corps.

6

10 THINGS YOU NEED TO KNOW ABOUT...

Ant-Man

7 The Microverse is a realm that Ant-Man can reach by shrinking to a tiny, subatomic size.

8 Both Hank and Scott have bonded with the ants they use, and have even named them. Lang's ants include Emma, Silver and Whitmore, while Pym befriended Crosby, Stills and Nash.

9 There has been a third Ant-Man – Eric O'Grady. This immoral S.H.I.E.L.D. agent steals the suit, but later tries to make up for his misdeeds by joining the Secret Avengers.

10 Scott Lang's daughter, Cassie, grows up to be a size-changing hero like her dad. She uses the identities Stature and Stinger.

BLACK PANTHER

T'Challa, the Black Panther, has to balance the two roles of King and Super Hero. He protects his people in Wakanda but also keeps the wider world safe from Super Villains.

1 What is the name of Black Panther's father?
   a. T'Challa   b. T'Chimi   c. T'Chassi   d. T'Chaka

2 What is the name of the plant that gives Black Panther his powers?
   a. Heart-shaped herb   c. Claw-shaped tree
   b. Cat-shaped shrub   d. Skull-shaped weed

3 Who are the elite soldiers who protect the Wakandan royal family?
   a. *Brenda Milaje*   c. *Dora Milaje*
   b. *Cat Clan*   d. *Mila Doraje*

4 Which of the X-Men is Black Panther married to for a time?
   a. Kitty Pryde   b. Emma Frost   c. Storm   d. Jean Grey

5 True or false? The villain Killmonger is T'Challa's brother.

6 Black Panther belonged to a secretive group of powerful geniuses who tried to prevent threats to Earth. What is its name?
   a. Illuminati   c. Hidden Heroes
   b. Covert Operators   d. Shhhhhhh!

7 Black Panther's costume is laced with which powerful substance?
a. Adamantium   b. Vibranium   c. Platinum   d. Venom

8 What is the name of the Panther Goddess, who makes sure Black Panther uses his powers only for good?
a. Panthra   c. Bast
b. Kandra   d. Dast

Genius Question
What is the name of Black Panther's sister?

9 True or false? Black Panther can access the knowledge of all the Black Panthers who have ever existed.

10 At which British university did T'Challa get a degree in Physics?
a. Oxford   c. Durham
b. Cambridge   d. Edinburgh

11 Black Panther once had to fight off an invasion of Wakanda by which other kingdom?
a. Kamar-Taj   c. Attilan
b. Transia   d. Atlantis

12 Which of these could not be used to describe Black Panther?
a. Expert tracker   c. Skilled martial artist
b. Genius inventor   d. Size-changer

13 True or false? Black Panther is a loner, preferring to face his enemies by himself.

ANSWERS

1d 2a 3c 4c 5 False – On Prime Earth, T'Challu's adoptive brother is the White Wolf.
6a 7b 8c 9 True – He was given this power by the Panther Goddess. 10a 11d 12d
13 False – Black Panther has been a member of several super-teams, including the Avengers.
Genius Question Shuri

Guardians of the Galaxy

TEAM-UP

The Guardians of the Galaxy are a group of weird and wonderful heroes who team up to battle cosmic bad guys.

Star-Lord

Half-human, half-alien Peter Quill is recruited by the space pirate Yondu. Trying to make his way in the universe, Peter calls himself Star-Lord and forms the Guardians of the Galaxy team.

Drax

Drax "The Destroyer" is dedicated to getting revenge on Thanos. He fights alone until he joins the Guardians of the Galaxy, who become a second family to him.

Gamora

Gamora is the adopted daughter of the evil Thanos, and is known as the Deadliest Woman in the Galaxy. She rejects her father's destructive ways and joins the Guardians to make the universe a better place.

Groot

A tree-like being from Planet X, Groot is extremely strong and can regrow himself from a tiny sprig. He has a special bond with Rocket.

Rocket Raccoon

Created in a lab on the planet Halfworld, Rocket is a creature resembling an Earth raccoon. Unlike regular raccoons, Rocket is a weapons expert and tactical genius.

HULK

You might not like him when he's angry, but how much do you know about the Avengers' powerhouse Hulk, a.k.a. Bruce Banner?

1 **What is it that first turns Bruce Banner into the Hulk?**
a. Alpha radiation
c. Gamma radiation
b. Beta radiation
d. Too much spinach

2 **What is Hulk's favourite word?**
a. Crush!
b. Smash!
c. Squish!
d. Splat!

3 **Who is the human that Bruce Banner is saving when he is transformed into Hulk?**
a. Rick Jones
c. Bucky Barnes
b. Amadeus Cho
d. General Ross

4 **Which emotion triggers Banner's transformation into the Hulk?**
a. Happiness
b. Sadness
c. Boredom
d. Anger

5 **Which planet did Hulk arrive on after being exiled from Earth for being too dangerous?**
a. Mars
b. Sakaar
c. Hala
d. Battleworld

6 **True or false? One of Hulk's nicknames is the Green Goliath.**

7 **True or false? Hulk was once a king.**

8 **True or false? Hulk has grey skin after his first transformation.**

9 What is the name of Bruce Banner's longtime love interest?
a. Sharon Carter   b. Pepper Potts   c. Betty Ross   d. Gwen Stacy

10 What relationship is Bruce Banner to She-Hulk Jen Walters?
a. Cousin   b. Brother   c. Father   d. Not related

11 Hulk has a son named Hiro-Kala. What is the name of Hulk's other son?
a. Junior   b. Tad   c. Greeny   d. Skaar

12 One of Hulk's worst enemies is another Hulk, but what colour is he?
a. Grey   b. Red   c. Purple   d. Pink

13 When Hulk becomes super-intelligent, what name does he go by?
a. Smart Hulk   c. Doc Green
b. Professor Smash   d. Big Brain

Genius Question
Which animal causes Hulk to revert back to human form?

14 Which Avenger does Bruce Banner ask to stop him if the Hulk ever gets out of control?
a. Hawkeye   c. Iron Man
b. Black Widow   d. Captain America

15 Which teenager transfers Hulk's power to himself to become a new Hulk?
a. Peter Parker   b. Sam Alexander   c. Kamala Khan   d. Amadeus Cho

16 What scientific field does genius Bruce Banner specialize in?
a. Chemistry   b. Nuclear physics   c. Biology   d. Astrophysics

ANSWERS

1c 2b 3a 4d 5b 6 True – Because he's green, and a giant like Goliath! 7 True – While on the planet Sakaar, he married its queen and ruled with her. 8 True – But the gamma radiation soon turns him green. 9c 10a 11d 12b 13c 14a 15d 16b **Genius Question** Puppies – he just can't stay angry around them!

25

5 THINGS YOU NEED TO KNOW ABOUT...

Squirrel Girl

1 Doreen Green is born with a long, fluffy tail like a squirrel's. She can also communicate with squirrels, has super-strength and agility, sharp teeth and claws.

2 Squirrel Girl's first squirrel sidekick is called Monkey Joe, who is later followed by Tippy-Toe.

3 Squirrel Girl has defeated Doctor Doom, the Abomination, Fin Fang Foom, Deadpool, M.O.D.O.K. – and Thanos!

4 Doreen is chosen to be the nanny for Danielle Cage, daughter of Luke Cage and Jessica Jones.

5 Squirrel Girl's secret weapon is her pack of cards – 4522 to be exact – created by Deadpool. They give her all the stats needed about the villains she faces.

TEAM-UP

Protectors of N.Y.C.

New York City always seems to be on the front line, whether against underworld villains or alien invaders. Luckily, it also has more than the average number of heroic protectors.

Hellcat
Patsy Walker is the super-powered Hellcat. She wears a cat costume that she can summon using the power of her mind.

White Tiger
Using the Amulets of Power, Ava Ayala has enhanced abilities and is a master of martial arts. She wields these skills as the hero White Tiger.

Misty Knight
Mercedes "Misty" Knight used to be a police officer. She is given a bionic arm by Tony Stark after being wounded in the line of duty. She sometimes teams up with the Defenders.

Iron Fist

Danny Rand is given the power of the Iron Fist after years training in martial arts in the mystical city of K'un-Lun. He returns to his native U.S.A. to use his power to protect the innocent.

Daredevil

Blindness has not stopped Matt Murdock becoming a successful lawyer – or a crime-fighting Super Hero. Enhanced senses help Matt protect his neighbourhood of Hell's Kitchen as Daredevil.

Jessica Jones

After a brief, unsuccessful career as the Super Hero Jewel, super-powered Jessica Jones becomes a private detective. Later she returns to heroics with husband Luke Cage.

Luke Cage

Super-strong, super-durable Luke Cage (formerly known as Power Man) forms the Defenders team with his friend Iron Fist, his wife Jessica Jones and N.Y.C.'s own Daredevil.

IMPOSSIBLE?
I've learned never to use that word in my line of work.

1. Doctor Stephen Strange is Earth's Sorcerer Supreme and a master of the mystical arts. Before that, he was one of the best surgeons in the world.

2. Doctor Strange is taught the ways of magic by an ancient mystic known as the Ancient One.

3. Strange lives in a very special house in Greenwich Village, New York City. It is known as his Sanctum Sanctorum.

7 Who is Thor's father?
a. Bor
b. Heimdall
c. Odin
d. Malekith

8 Before picking up his hammer, Thor wielded Jarnbjorn. What type of weapon was it?
a. Axe
b. Spear
c. Staff
d. Mace

9 Thor is a founding member of which super-team?
a. X-Men
b. Guardians of the Galaxy
c. Alpha Flight
d. Avengers

10 In which country on Earth was Thor born?
a. Norway
b. U.S.A.
c. Australia
d. Canada

11 True or false? Thor has fought a monster big enough to encircle the world.

12 Who was Thor's childhood friend and first love?
a. Jane Foster
b. Lady Sif
c. Black Widow
d. Pepper Potts

13 What is the name of the alien who proved worthy enough to lift Thor's hammer?
a. Alpha Ray Alan
b. Beta Ray Bill
c. Gamma Ray Greg
d. Delta Ray Dave

14 To maintain his immortality, Thor must eat an enchanted version of which fruit?
a. Oranges
b. Bananas
c. Apples
d. Peaches

15 The Pet Avengers' roster includes a version of Thor. What animal is he?
a. Frog
b. Dog
c. Cat
d. Falcon

16 Who took up the mantle of Thor when he became unworthy to wield his hammer?
a. Jane Foster
b. Tony Stark
c. Loki
d. Bruce Banner

ANSWERS

1a 2d 3c 4a 5 False – Thor is the god of thunder. 6b 7c 8a 9d 10a
11 True – The Midgard Serpent. 12b 13b 14c 15a 16a
Genius Question Ragnarok

33

TEAM-UP

Inhumans

Meet the Inhumans — a subspecies of human, genetically engineered to have amazing abilities.

Crystal
Medusa's sister, Crystal, has powers over the four elements of fire, air, water and earth. She can use her powers to fly, and can also create earthquakes or tidal waves.

Triton
The brother of Karnak, Triton can only survive underwater, or by using special breathing equipment.

Maximus
Black Bolt's brother is resentful of Black Bolt's power and often plots against him. He has mind-control abilities and is often called Maximus the Mad.

Black Bolt

The King of the Inhumans is mostly silent, as his voice is a hugely destructive weapon. Black Bolt's real name is Blackagar Boltagon.

Karnak

Karnak is a master martial artist, as well as a priest and philosopher. He has the power to shatter almost any substance, or render even very strong beings unconscious.

Medusa

Medusa is Queen of the Inhumans. Her power is found in her long hair, which can reach out and trap enemies, or be used as a whiplike weapon.

Gorgon

Gorgon Petragon can create huge shockwaves by stamping his hoof-like feet. He is the cousin of Black Bolt and Maximus.

Lockjaw

The Inhumans' dog is not just a family pet. Lockjaw has the ability of teleportation, and the Inhumans use him to travel around. He is also a member of the Pet Avengers.

35

16,649°C

Heat of the infrared beam (30,000°F) Vision emits from the solar gem on his forehead. This cool android can be a real hothead!

WOW!

38,624kph

Approximate speed Thor can fly (24,000mph).

1.3cm

Janet Van Dyne's height as Wasp (0.5in).

122

The number of arrow types Hawkeye uses (there could be even more – it's tough for him to keep count!)

1922

The year Steve Rogers was born.

100

... and counting! Wolverine's age.

WHAM!

150,000,000,000

The weight in tonnes of the mountain range Molecule Man drops on the Hulk! The Hulk catches it – proving he's an unbelievable powerhouse!

15m

The maximum distance Daredevil can track a person by smell through a crowd (50ft).

NUMBER CRUNCH

There is no better way of learning how Super Heroes are so amazing than by looking at their most mind-boggling stats!

96.6kph

Namor the Sub-Mariner's top swimming speed (60mph). This is over 13 times quicker than the fastest human swimmer.

30.5m

Hank Pym's max size as Goliath/Giant-Man (100ft).

457m

Maximum length (1,500ft) that Mister Fantastic can stretch part of his body.

3000

Active S.H.I.E.L.D agents prior to the superhuman civil war.

YAY!

10,000+

The number of lives Spidey has probably saved.

12,348kph

The speed that Iron Man's Space Armour MK III can reach (7,673mph).

X-MEN

There is no doubt that the mutant powers of the X-Men make them some of the most amazing heroes on the planet. Are you up to speed with all the X-knowledge?

True or False?

1 The original team assembled by Professor X is Cyclops, Beast, Iceman, Angel and Marvel Girl.

2 Professor X's mutant power is creating powerful blasts of electricity.

3 The first villain faced by the X-Men is Apocalypse.

4 Celestials are giant robots programmed to catch mutants like the X-Men.

5 Charles Xavier's stepbrother is a mutant Super Villain.

6 Rogue's alter ego is Ororo Munroe.

7 Storm meets Professor X when she tries to steal from him.

8 Jean Grey turns from good to evil.

9 Cyclops and Havok are brothers.

10 After transforming into Beast, Hank McCoy loses his genius intelligence.

11 X-Men Cable and Bishop are both from the future.

12 X-Man Angel was once one of the scary Horsemen of the Apocalypse.

13 Colossus has size-changing abilities.

14 Nightcrawler is from Russia.

15 Kitty Pryde has also been a Guardian of the Galaxy.

16 Rogue can absorb the power of others.

17 Kitty Pryde has a pet dragon.

18 Emma Frost's powers enable her to freeze things.

19 Psylocke is the wife of Captain Britain.

20 Gambit's weapon of choice is a playing card.

21 The mutant Goldballs fires gold balls from his body.

ANSWERS

1 True – But many more would join them!

2 False – Charles Xavier can read and influence the minds of others.

3 False – It is Magneto, master of magnetism.

4 False – The mutant-hunting robots are Sentinels.

5 True – He is the mighty Juggernaut.

6 False – Ororo is Storm.

7 True – Although she did not know she was a mutant at the time.

8 True – She becomes the powerful and destructive Dark Phoenix.

9 True – And there is another Summers sibling, Gabriel, a.k.a. Vulcan.

10 False – Beast remains one of the most intelligent people on Earth.

11 True – They have a unique insight into present-day events.

12 True – But he is now back on the side of good.

13 False – He can turn his body into organic steel.

14 False – He is German.

15 True – She is a key part of any team she joins.

16 True – She only has to touch them.

17 True – His name is Lockheed.

18 False – She is a powerful telepath.

19 False – She is his sister.

20 True – He charges them up with energy before throwing them.

21 True – Strange but true!

WOLVERINE

He's the best there is at what he does, but are you the best there is at knowing Wolverine's most important facts?

1 Which country does Wolverine come from?
a. U.K.   b. Australia   c. Canada   d. U.S.A.

2 Which super-strong substance are his claws made of?
a. Adamantium   b. Vibranium   c. Steel   d. Uru

3 What is the name of Wolverine's nemesis?
a. Badger   b. Sabretooth   c. Raccoon   d. Grizzly

4 He likes to be called Logan, but what is Wolverine's real name?
a. Scott Summers   c. Remy LeBeau
b. Kurt Wagner   d. James Howlett

5 True or false? Wolverine has a son.

6 True or false? Wolverine is more than 100 years old.

7 What is the name of the top-secret program that enhanced Wolverine's natural mutant abilities?
a. Weapon Q   b. Weapon X   c. Weapon Y   d. Weapon Z

8 Wolverine has a young female clone, code-named X-23. What is her name?

a. Laura Kinney   b. Kara Linney   c. Sara Smith   d. Paula Phillips

9 Which of these super-teams has Wolverine belonged to?

a. Avengers
b. X-Men
c. Fantastic Four
d. All of the above

10 True or false? Wolverine can speak Japanese.

11 What is Wolverine's favourite sport?

a. Basketball   c. Ice hockey
b. Baseball   d. Football

12 Wolverine is the founder of which institution?

a. Xavier's School for Gifted Youngsters
b. Jean Grey School for Higher Learning
c. Hellfire Club
d. Avengers Academy

Genius Question
What noise do Wolverine's claws make when he springs them from his hands?

13 Which of his fellow X-Men does Wolverine have a major crush on?

a. Jean Grey   c. Rogue
b. Kitty Pryde d. Psylocke

14 True or false? No weapon on Earth can harm Wolverine, thanks to his healing factor.

ANSWERS

1 c **2** a **3** b **4** d **5** True – Named Daken, Wolverine's son has not turned out well. **6** True – He was born in 1880, but his healing factor slows his ageing. **7** b **8** a **9** d **10** True – Along with many other languages. **11** c **12** b **13** a **14** False – His healing factor does not work against the mystical Muramasa Blade. **Genius Question** Snikt!

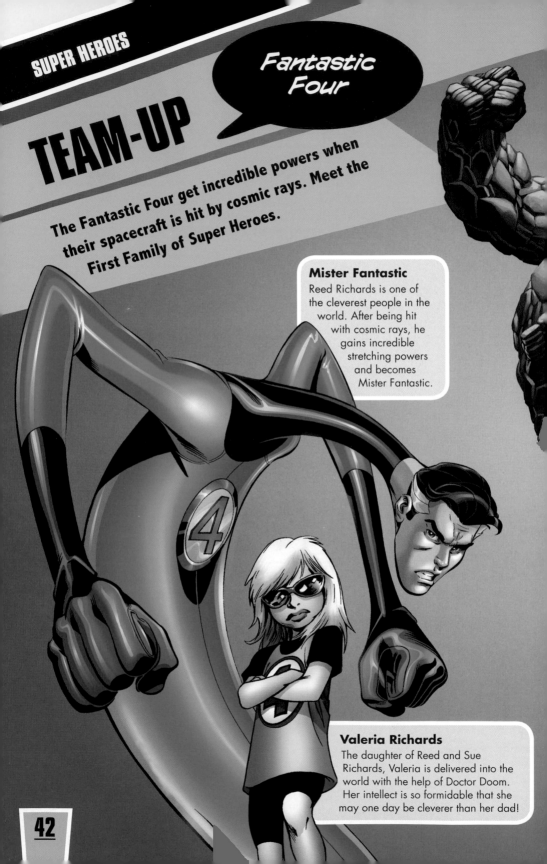

Fantastic Four

TEAM-UP

The Fantastic Four get incredible powers when their spacecraft is hit by cosmic rays. Meet the First Family of Super Heroes.

Mister Fantastic

Reed Richards is one of the cleverest people in the world. After being hit with cosmic rays, he gains incredible stretching powers and becomes Mister Fantastic.

Valeria Richards

The daughter of Reed and Sue Richards, Valeria is delivered into the world with the help of Doctor Doom. Her intellect is so formidable that she may one day be cleverer than her dad!

The Thing
Reed Richards' best friend Ben Grimm is a test pilot who drives the team on their fateful space flight. He turns into a super-strong creature with rock-like skin.

Invisible Woman
Sue Storm Richards can make herself invisible, and can create powerful force fields. She has often been the glue holding the FF together during troubled times.

Human Torch
Sue's brother Johnny Storm is the Human Torch. He is able to fly and can turn his body into flames. When not fighting bad guys, he loves fixing up and driving cars.

Franklin Richards
Reed and Sue's eldest child is born a mutant with incredible psionic powers. His powers are so great that he can create new realities.

ACROSS THE UNIVERSE

Heroes do not have to be from Earth – there's a multiverse of powerful aliens out there! How much do you know about cosmic beings?

True or False?

1 The powerful Silver Surfer is originally called Norrin Radd.

2 The hero Mar-Vell belonged to the alien Skrull race.

3 Shi'ar ruler Lilandra once married one of the X-Men.

4 Lilandra is the leader of the space pirates known as the Starjammers.

5 The Nova Corps are based on the planet Hala.

6 Several Earth humans have been members of the Nova Corps.

7 Kree-Skrull hybrid Teddy Altman goes by the hero codename Hulkling.

Nova

8 Lilandra has to fight her own sister after she becomes a villain.

9 Uatu the Watcher observes Earth from the planet Mars.

10 Xavin – a rare good Skrull – belongs to the Runaways team.

11 Mar-Vell, the original Captain Marvel, has no children.

12 Noh-Varr is also known as Marvel Boy.

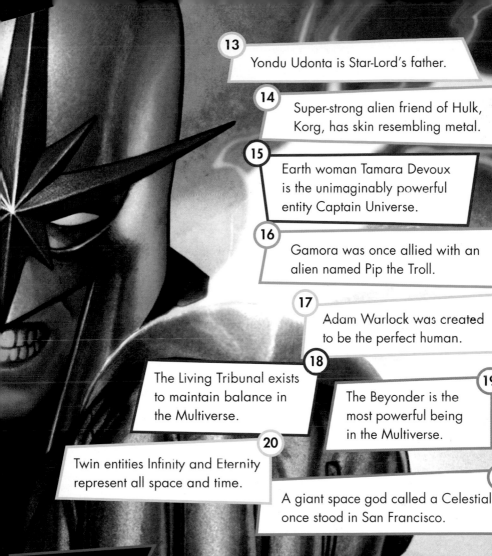

13 Yondu Udonta is Star-Lord's father.

14 Super-strong alien friend of Hulk, Korg, has skin resembling metal.

15 Earth woman Tamara Devoux is the unimaginably powerful entity Captain Universe.

16 Gamora was once allied with an alien named Pip the Troll.

17 Adam Warlock was created to be the perfect human.

18 The Living Tribunal exists to maintain balance in the Multiverse.

19 The Beyonder is the most powerful being in the Multiverse.

20 Twin entities Infinity and Eternity represent all space and time.

21 A giant space god called a Celestial once stood in San Francisco.

ANSWERS

1 True – He comes from the planet Zenn-La.
2 False – Mar-Vell was a Kree.
3 True – She married Charles Xavier, a.k.a. Professor X.
4 False – The Starjammers are led by Corsair, father to the mutants Cyclops, Havok and Vulcan.
5 False – Their home is Xandar – it is the Kree who are from Hala.

6 True – Richard Rider and Sam Alexander are the most famous of the Earth Novas.
7 True – His mixed heritage has given him some amazing powers.
8 True – Lilandra's sister is the evil Deathbird.
9 False – Uatu is based on Earth's Moon.
10 True – Xavin uses Skrull shape-shifting powers to do good.
11 False – He has three: Genis-Vell, Phyla-Vell and Hulkling.

12 True – He is a Kree from an alternate universe.
13 False – But he does take the young man into his Ravagers gang.
14 False – Korg's skin is like rock.
15 True – She is chosen as a partner for the universal energy while in a coma.
16 True – Pip is from the planet Laxidazia.
17 True – At that time he was known only as "Him".

18 True – This ancient entity has limitless power.
19 False – The being that created the Multiverse, known as the One-Above-All, is the most powerful.
20 True – They have the power to manipulate any force or energy in the Multiverse.
21 True – The 610m (2000ft) "statue" became quite a tourist attraction!

7 THINGS YOU NEED TO KNOW ABOUT...

Moon Girl

1 Moon Girl's real name is Lunella Lafayette. She is a nine-year-old girl who goes to school in New York.

2 Even at her young age, Moon Girl is extraordinarily clever. She invents a host of gadgets, including armour and weapons.

3 Devil Dinosaur is Moon Girl's crime fighting partner. He is an intelligent beast who closely resembles a Tyrannosaurus rex.

4 Moon Girl has Inhuman DNA. After being exposed to Terrigen Mists, she develops the power to swap her mind into the body of Devil Dinosaur.

5 Moon Girl's ability to swap bodies with Devil Dinosaur manifests when she is feeling a strong emotion – or when she is hungry!

STRANGE HEROES

The world needs heroes that are fully equipped to deal with weird and supernatural threats — small wonder that they can be a little strange themselves!

Man-Thing

1 What is mass-increasing **HERO** Big Bertha's day job?

a. Waitress
b. Schoolteacher
c. Supermodel
d. Reporter

2 **TRUE OR FALSE?**

Mr Immortal, leader of the Great Lakes Avengers, cannot be killed.

In which landscape does Ted Sallis become **MAN-THING**?

3
a. Swamp
b. Desert
c. Jungle
d. Mountains

Genius Question

Which monster hunter got his name from the mystical gem that gave him his powers 10,000 years ago?

4 Man-Thing shares his Everglades home with which **MYSTICAL GATEWAY**?

a. The Magic Door
b. The Nexus of All Realities
c. The Link
d. Reality Gap

TRUE OR FALSE?
Like the Ghost Riders who went before him, Robbie Reyes rides a motorcycle.

 TRUE OR FALSE?
The hero Gwenpool has exceptional knowledge of Super Heroes and Villains.

 Robbie Reyes as Ghost Rider is possessed by a **SPIRIT**. What is its name?
a. Bob   c. Eli
b. Gwen   d. Ben

 What is the **CODENAME** of **STEVE HARMON**, who is transformed into a living cartoon character?
a. Clown Boy
b. Slapstick
c. Loon Lad
d. Crazy Cat

 Which **MARTIAL ART** does Howard the Duck practise?
a. Duck Fu   c. Karategg
b. Quak Fu   d. Ju-ducksu

 And which cartoon-like **WEAPON** does he use?
a. Trick flower
b. One-ton weight
c. Giant boxing glove
d. Oversized mallet

 What is Howard the Duck's **JOB**?
a. Chef
b. Teacher
c. Doctor
d. Private investigator

 Which supernatural **CREATURES** does Blade specialise in hunting?
a. Vampires
b. Zombies
c. Witches
d. Werewolves

 X-Men ally Doop's **BRAIN** once exploded. Luckily he has a second one, but where?
a. His arm
b. In a box
c. His hindquarters
d. His stomach

 What is Blade's preferred **WEAPON**?
a. Laser gun   c. Sword
b. Crossbow   d. Axe

 What is the **VAMPIRIC HELLCOW'S** real name?
a. Bessie   c. Maisy
b. Daisy   d. Moora

TEAM-UP

S.H.I.E.L.D.

S.H.I.E.L.D. (Strategic Homeland Intervention, Enforcement and Logistics Division) is an organisation set up to protect the world from evil. Although most agents are not super-powered, they are brave and dedicated to their mission.

Maria Hill

Tough agent Maria Hill succeeds Nick Fury as S.H.I.E.L.D. director. She is naturally suspicious of superhumans, and her methods sometimes bring her into conflict with heroes like the Avengers.

Nick Fury

Natural soldier Nick Fury has years of covert ops under his belt when he is chosen as the new director of S.H.I.E.L.D. He is not afraid to make tough choices if he believes it will protect humanity.

Dum-Dum Dugan
Timothy "Dum-Dum" Dugan is a close friend and wartime comrade of Nick Fury. When Fury joins S.H.I.E.L.D., Dugan joins too as his right-hand man. He wears a distinctive bowler hat.

Phil Coulson
One of Nick Fury, Jr's Rangers buddies, Coulson is a big fan of Super Heroes. He is delighted to join S.H.I.E.L.D. and get the chance to fight alongside his idols.

Nick Fury, Jr
U.S. Ranger Marcus Johnson discovers that he is really the son of Nick Fury. He joins S.H.I.E.L.D. as Nick Fury, Jr, specialising in superhuman operations.

Sharon Carter
Sharon is inspired to join S.H.I.E.L.D. by her Aunt Peggy, a hero of the resistance during World War II. Code named Agent 13, Sharon Carter is a highly trained fighter and sharpshooter.

1 What relation is Namora to Namor?
a. Sister
b. Daughter
c. Mother
d. Cousin

2 Which hero is said to have the power of a million exploding suns?
a. Sentry
b. Wonder Man
c. Deathlok
d. Punisher

3 True or false? She-Hulk was once a member of the Fantastic Four.

4 True or false? Namor has romantic feelings for Black Widow.

5 At which college did She-Hulk Jennifer Walters get her law degree?
a. Harvard
b. Berkeley
c. NYU
d. UCLA

6 What sort of vehicle does the Punisher transport his weapons and equipment in?
a. Car
b. Motorcycle and sidecar
c. Van
d. Helicopter

She-Hulk

7 Which evil ninja organisation did Elektra infiltrate and train with?
a. The Foot
b. The Hand
c. The Arm
d. The Head

Genius Question

What cyborg codename has been used by Luther Manning, Michael Collins and Henry Hayes, among others?

EXTREME HEROES

When faced with the toughest bad guys, you need the toughest heroes, those who are not afraid to break a few rules – or a few noses – to get the job done.

8 True or false? The Sentry's power comes from a version of the Super-Soldier Serum that created Captain America.

9 Who is the Punisher sworn to take revenge on?
a. Spider-Man
b. Gangsters
c. Skrulls
d. Shop lifters

10 What is Deadpool's nickname?
a. The Funny Assassin
b. Killer Clown
c. Grinning Gunslinger
d. Merc with a Mouth

11 True or false? The assassin Elektra is originally from Greece.

12 Namor the Sub-Mariner is king of which undersea kingdom?
a. Pacificia
b. Artica
c. Thera
d. Atlantis

13 What is the alter ego of Marc Spector, who believes his powers come from an Egyptian god?
a. Sun King
b. Moon Knight
c. Star-Lord
d. Captain Comet

14 When Agent Venom becomes Agent Anti-Venom, what colour is his suit?
a. Red
b. White
c. Black
d. Green

15 Which of Peter Parker's old friends becomes Agent Venom?
a. Harry Osborn
b. Betty Brant
c. Flash Thompson
d. Mary Jane Watson

16 What is the alter ego of Deadpool?
a. Wade Wilson
b. Sam Wilson
c. Wilson Fisk
d. Cade Wilson

ANSWERS

1d **2**a **3** True – She replaced the Thing in the line-up while he explored space. **4** False – But he has always had a soft spot for the Fantastic Four's Suc Storm. **5**d **6**c **7**b **8** True – But the Sentry's version was thousands of times stronger. **9**b **10**d **11** True – She came to the U.S.A. to go to college. **12**d **13**b **14**b **15**c **16**a **Genius Question** Deathlok

5 THINGS YOU NEED TO KNOW ABOUT...

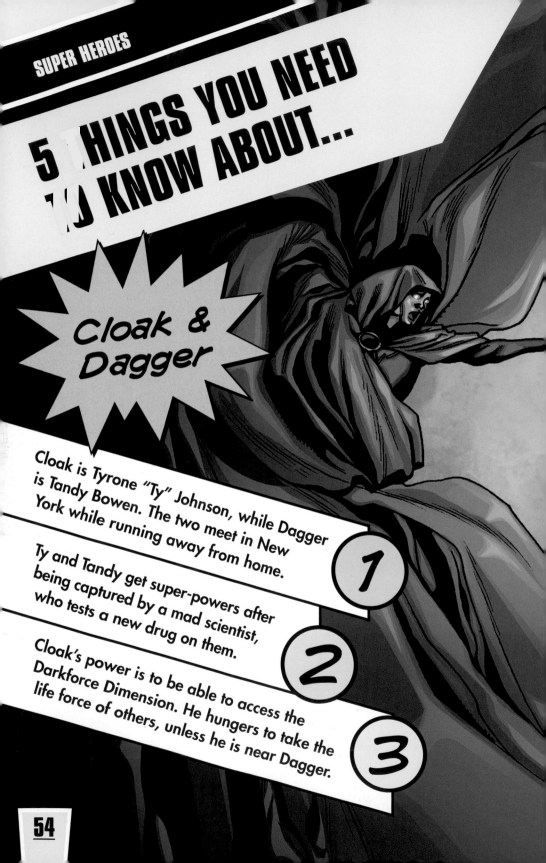

Cloak & Dagger

Cloak is Tyrone "Ty" Johnson, while Dagger is Tandy Bowen. The two meet in New York while running away from home. **1**

Ty and Tandy get super-powers after being captured by a mad scientist, who tests a new drug on them. **2**

Cloak's power is to be able to access the Darkforce Dimension. He hungers to take the life force of others, unless he is near Dagger. **3**

TEAM-UP

Runaways

What would you do if you found out your parents were Super Villains? The Runaways decide to form a super-team and try and make up for the bad behaviour of their fathers and mothers.

1 Nico Minoru

The daughter of dark wizards, Nico is able to use magic when she summons the powerful Staff of One. She can fly, teleport and move things with her mind.

2 Chase Stein

High-school jock Chase is the only member of the Runaways with a driver's licence. He has no powers, but arms himself with tech stolen from his evil parents, including X-ray goggles and Fistigons – gloves that blast out lightning, missiles, or fire.

3 Karolina Dean

Karolina discovers that she is really an alien – a Majesdanian who can absorb energy from the sun and radiate it in rainbow-coloured light. She can channel the energy into blasts or force fields.

4 Gertrude Yorkes

Gert is questioning and outspoken. She has a telepathic link to a genetically engineered dinosaur called Old Lace, brought from the future by her time-travelling parents.

5 Molly Hayes

The youngest member of the Runaways is also the strongest. Molly is a mutant with incredible super-strength and durability.

6 Victor Mancha

Son of evil robot Ultron, Victor is a cyborg Super Hero whose body has been destroyed. Victor is quite happy living as just a head and lets Molly style his hair.

Old Lace

57

TEAMS

If there's one thing stronger than a Super Hero, it's a team of Super Heroes. Are you clued up on the greatest team-ups of all time?

True or False?

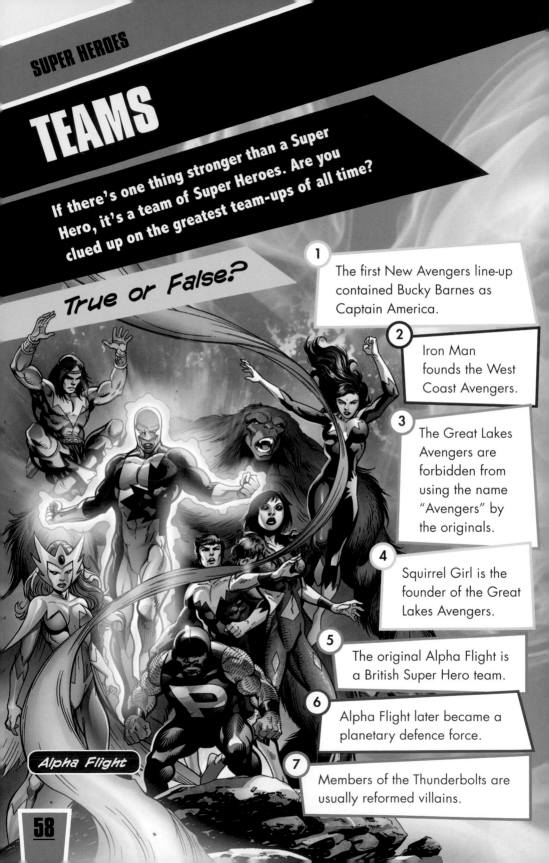

Alpha Flight

1 The first New Avengers line-up contained Bucky Barnes as Captain America.

2 Iron Man founds the West Coast Avengers.

3 The Great Lakes Avengers are forbidden from using the name "Avengers" by the originals.

4 Squirrel Girl is the founder of the Great Lakes Avengers.

5 The original Alpha Flight is a British Super Hero team.

6 Alpha Flight later became a planetary defence force.

7 Members of the Thunderbolts are usually reformed villains.

8 Cloak and Dagger team up after being turned into superhumans by a criminal gang.

9 Cloak's dark powers are kept under control by Dagger's light.

10 The original Heroes for Hire are Luke Cage and Jessica Jones.

11 Mercs for Money is led by Hawkeye.

12 Members of the Squadron Supreme come from different time periods.

13 The Runaways are all the children of Super Heroes.

14 The Champions is a team of dissatisfied former Avengers.

15 The Champions are led by Nova.

16 X-Force is a mutant team willing to be more aggressive than the X-Men.

17 The Future Foundation is a team of brilliant minds assembled by Tony Stark.

18 Excalibur is a team based in Britain.

19 West Coast Avengers is formed from the remains of the Force Works team.

20 The aim of Force Works is to prevent disasters rather than react to them.

21 The original Defenders were Doctor Strange, Hulk and Namor.

ANSWERS

1 False – Bucky was on the roster of a later lineup.
2 False – It is Hawkeye.
3 True – So the team tries being the Great Lakes X-Men instead.
4 False – It is Mister Immortal, although Squirrel Girl is later a member.
5 False – Alpha Flight is Canadian.
6 True – Led by Captain Marvel, it guards against alien threats.

7 True – Although some are more reformed than others.
8 True – Their mission is to stop criminals like those who gave them their powers.
9 True – This team has a very special bond, and their powers are linked.
10 False – It is Luke Cage and Iron Fist.
11 False – It is Deadpool.
12 False – They are from different universes.

13 False – The Runaways' parents are villains.
14 True – The current version of the group wants to do things their own way.
15 False – Ms Marvel is the Champions' leader.
16 True – They are led by Cable.
17 False – It is Reed Richards who creates the Future Foundation.

18 True – It is led by Captain Britain but has featured heroes of many nationalities.
19 False – Force Works is formed from the West Coast Avengers.
20 True – Tony Stark creates the team to have a different outlook on saving people.
21 True – This "non-team" comprised some heavy hitters!

59

Venom

VILLAINS

Meet the biggest, baddest villains around! They can be mad scientists, powerful aliens or dangerous gangsters, but all of them are up to ne good!

MAD, BAD AND DANGEROUS TO KNOW

Some villains have strange powers, odd appearances or crazy plans… And some have all of the above!

1 What is the villain Kang's nickname?
a. The Conqueror
b. The Bad
c. The Naughty
d. The Fluffy

3 Kang's battle armour makes his face appear to be which colour?
a. Red
b. Yellow
c. Silver
d. Blue

2 What ability is Kang best known for?
a. Light-speed space travel
b. Mind-controlling animals
c. Time travel
d. Imitating the powers of others

5 True or false? Dormammu's daughter falls in love with his nemesis Doctor Strange.

4 Ruler of the Dark Dimension Dormammu usually appears surrounded by what?
a. Puppies
b. Flowers
c. Flames
d. Lightning blasts

6 Why does Baron Heinrich Zemo never remove his mask?
a. His identity is super-secret
b. It is stuck on with indestructible glue
c. He hates the smell of the outside world
d. He just loves the colour too much

7 Who is Baron Zemo's most hated foe?
a. Captain America
b. Iron Man
c. Scarlet Witch
d. Black Widow

8 What is the name of the evil team created by Baron Zemo?
a. The Ze-monsters
b. Masters of Evil
c. The Baron's Baddies
d. The Revengers

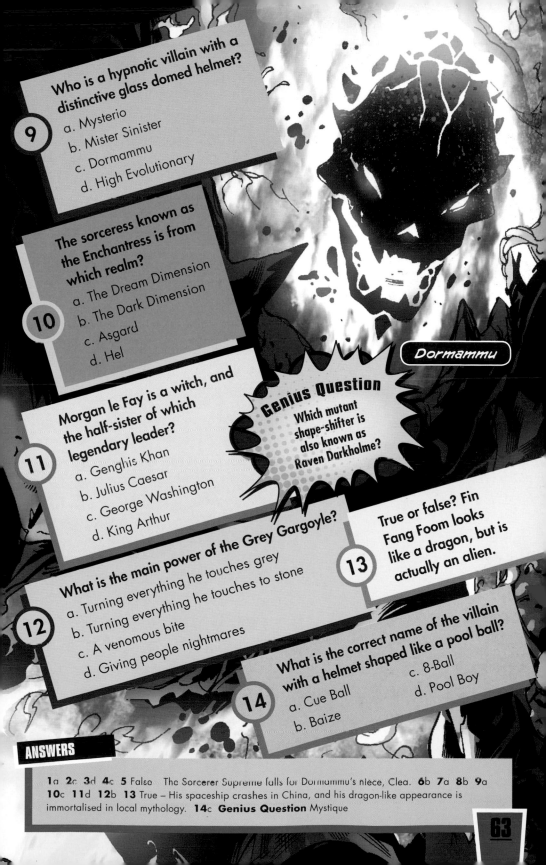

9 Who is a hypnotic villain with a distinctive glass domed helmet?

a. Mysterio
b. Mister Sinister
c. Dormammu
d. High Evolutionary

10 The sorceress known as the Enchantress is from which realm?

a. The Dream Dimension
b. The Dark Dimension
c. Asgard
d. Hel

Dormammu

11 Morgan le Fay is a witch, and the half-sister of which legendary leader?

a. Genghis Khan
b. Julius Caesar
c. George Washington
d. King Arthur

Genius Question
Which mutant shape-shifter is also known as Raven Darkholme?

12 What is the main power of the Grey Gargoyle?

a. Turning everything he touches grey
b. Turning everything he touches to stone
c. A venomous bite
d. Giving people nightmares

13 True or false? Fin Fang Foom looks like a dragon, but is actually an alien.

14 What is the correct name of the villain with a helmet shaped like a pool ball?

a. Cue Ball
b. Baize
c. 8-Ball
d. Pool Boy

ANSWERS

1a 2c 3d 4c 5 False The Sorcerer Supreme falls for Dormammu's niece, Clea. 6b 7a 8b 9a
10c 11d 12b 13 True – His spaceship crashes in China, and his dragon-like appearance is
immortalised in local mythology. 14c **Genius Question** Mystique

10 THINGS YOU NEED TO KNOW ABOUT...

Loki

1 He is the adopted brother of Thor.

2 He is the self-proclaimed god of mischief.

3 His birth parents are Frost Giants of Jotunheim.

4 He has died and been reborn as the child "Kid Loki".

5 He possesses magical powers, including the ability to shape-shift.

6 Loki was once reborn as a woman, taking the form of Lady Sif.

7 Loki's full name is Loki Laufeyson.

MAD SCIENTISTS

Unfortunately some of the world's most intelligent people have chosen to use their genius for evil. Take A.I.M. at these mad scientist questions!

1 Which century was unscrupulous biologist Mister Sinister born in?
a. 19th
c. 21st
b. 20th
d. 25th

2 Which powerful villain was awoken by Mister Sinister?
a. Magneto
c. Thanos
b. Apocalypse
d. Dark Beast

3 True or false? The High Evolutionary has built a replica of Earth.

4 By what alter ego is biochemist Miles Warren better known?
a. Lizard
b. Doctor Octopus
c. Jackal
d. Carnage

5 Who does Miles Warren fall in love with and clone in his lab?
a. Gwen Stacy
b. Mary Jane Watson
c. Betty Brant
d. Liz Allan

Mister Sinister

Genius Question
What is the name of the scientist who builds the mutant-hunting Sentinel robots?

6 What is the name of the robot created by the Mad Thinker?
a. Radical Robot
b. Awesome Android
c. Cool Cyborg
d. Marvellous Mechanoid

7 Where does the Mad Thinker's robot creation work after it breaks free of his control?
a. Stark Industries
b. A.I.M.
c. She-Hulk's law firm
d. Midtown High

8 What are the New Men, created by the High Evolutionary?
a. Humanoid animals
b. Two-headed humans
c. Giants
d. People who age backwards

9 What is the name of the mountain in Transia where the High Evolutionary has his lab?
a. Blunderbus
b. Dumbledore
c. Grocerystore
d. Wundagore

10 Which scientist accidentally glued his mask to his face – permanently?
a. Arnim Zola
b. Baron Zemo
c. Spencer Smythe
d. Mister Sinister

11 True or false? Arnim Zola has invented a way to live forever.

12 True or false? A.I.M. stands for All Ideas Malicious.

13 True or false? The Tinkerer makes weapons and equipment for his fellow bad guys.

ANSWERS

1a 2b 3 True – It is called Counter-Earth and it is on a solar orbit directly opposite that of Earth, so it can never be seen. 4c 5a 6b
7c 8a 9d 10b 11 True – He has downloaded his consciousness into a robot body. 12 False – It's Advanced Idea Mechanics.
13 True—He made or improved Mysterio's suit, Scorpion's tail and Rocket Racer's skateboard, among others!
Genius Question Dr Bolivar Trask

ZOOM!

299,792

The speed Living Laser can travel in kilometres per second (186,282 miles per second).

192

The number of words the alien Chitauri have for "hate".

113kph

Lizard's tail whip speed (70mph).

483kph

Top speed of the Green Goblin's glider (300mph).

5,000

Age of the villainous Sphinx.

WHAT!?

100,000,000

The estimated total of people killed by Thanos – but the number could be even higher!

800

Number of years the shadowy Atlas Foundation has existed. It was founded by followers of legendary warrior Genghis Khan!

NUMBER CRUNCH

If you want to know what makes the villains of the Marvel Universe so scary, take a look at their stats! No wonder only the mightiest of heroes can defeat them!

340kg

Weight of evil human supercomputer M.O.D.O.K. (750lb).

4.8km

Height of evil alien Apocalypse Beast (3 miles).

6,978

Number of heroes defeated by Ultron in the alternate reality Age of Ultron. The remaining heroes have to travel back in time to stop Ultron's rule before it happens!

OH!

$1 million

Reward offered by *The Daily Bugle* on behalf of Norman Osborn for the capture of Spider-Man.

50

The weight in tonnes that Loki can lift.

5 THINGS YOU NEED TO KNOW ABOUT...

Hydra

1 Hydra is a secretive evil organisation whose goal is world domination.

2 Hydra operatives traditionally wear green uniforms with a large, yellow letter H on the front.

3 The Hydra symbol is a skull with six tentacles coming out of it.

4 Hydra is named after a mythical, many-headed beast faced by the hero Hercules. When one of its heads was cut off, two more would grow in its place.

5 The leader of Hydra is called the Supreme Hydra. Former Supreme Hydras include Baron von Strucker, Viper, Red Skull and even a Cosmic Cube-created Captain America!

THANOS

Thanos is one of the most dangerous beings in the universe. Tread carefully as you find out how much you know about the ultimate bad guy.

1 Where is Thanos from?
a. Earth   b. Titan   c. Hala   d. The Moon

2 Which powerful entity is Thanos always trying to impress?
a. Galactus   b. The Beyonder   c. Death   d. Ego the Living Planet

3 Which cosmic menace did Thanos team up with when he got bored?
a. Magus   b. The Kree   c. The Brood   d. Annihilus

4 Which of these Guardians of the Galaxy has sworn revenge on Thanos?
a. Drax   b. Rocket   c. Groot   d. Star-Lord

5 Thanos once belonged to which Super Hero team?
a. Avengers
b. Guardians of the Galaxy
c. Infinity Watch
d. Alpha Flight

6 Which of Earth's heroes succeeds in imprisoning Thanos?
a. Iron Man
b. War Machine
c. Captain Marvel
d. Spider-Man

7 Which of these is not a member of Thanos' deadly Black Order?
a. Proxima Centauri
b. Ebony Maw
c. Corvus Glaive
d. Supergiant

8 True or false? Thanos has a son called Thane.

9 True or false? Thanos destroys his homeworld.

10 True or false? Thanos has a brother allied with the Avengers.

11 Which is the correct name of one of Thanos' most frequent foes?
a. Ethan Airlock
c. Callum Sherlock
b. Adam Warlock
d. William Warlock

12 What does Thanos wear to wield the incredible power of the Infinity Stones?
a. Infinity Hat
c. Infinity Belt
b. Infinity Gauntlet
d. Infinity Sock

13 True or false? Thanos is descended from the ancient and powerful Celestials.

14 On one occasion, Thanos is defeated by his granddaughter. What is her name?
a. Gamora
c. Ayesha
b. Death
d. Nebula

15 What is the name of Thanos' starship?
a. Deathbird
c. Big Blue
b. Sanctuary II
d. Titanic

Genius Question

What is the name of Thanos' adopted daughter, whom he raised to be the deadliest woman in the galaxy?

16 Why does Thanos want the Cosmic Cube?
a. To help him control the universe
b. He likes shiny things
c. To defeat the Avengers
d. To annoy the Guardians of the Galaxy

ANSWERS

1b 2c 3d 4a 5c 6c 7a 8 True – But Thanos is not interested in being a good dad!
9 True – Thanos has no more affection for his home than any of the other planets he attacks.
10 True – Starfox is very different from his scary brother! 11b 12b 13 False – Thanos is descended from the Eternals. 14d 15b 16a **Genius Question** Gamora

TEAM-UP

Black Order

Thanos' most loyal followers are the elite Black Order, also known as the Cull Obsidian. You'd better hope they don't visit your planet!

Corvus Glaive
Thanos' right-hand man, Corvus Glaive wields a blade that can cut through atoms. He is immortal as long as his blade remains unbroken.

Supergiant
Supergiant is a powerful telepath and mind-controller whose abilities work on any species she encounters. She is killed during the Black Order's attempted takeover of Earth.

Black Dwarf
Black Dwarf is brother to Corvus Glaive. He is super-strong, with unbreakable skin and his preferred weapon is a double-bladed axe.

Proxima Midnight

A powerful warrior of Thanos, Proxima Midnight is armed with a spear of incredible power, forged from a sun that is suspended between the states of star, supernova and black hole.

Ebony Maw

Perhaps the most dangerous of the Black Order, Ebony Maw can persuade beings to do his bidding just by whispering in their ear. He is a master tactician.

Thanos

Even a being as mighty as Thanos needs lieutenants to help him achieve his terrible ambitions. Thanos assembles some of the most evil entities in the universe to be his elite corps.

Black Swan

This mysterious character at first seems to be trying to help save the universe. However, after order is restored she becomes a servant of Thanos in his new Black Order.

EXTRATERRESTRIAL MENACES

The universe is a dangerous place, especially if you run into one of these cosmic bad guys. Are you an extraterrestrial expert?

True or False?

1 The Brood are insectoid beings who lay their eggs on their prey.

2 The Brood operate a hive system led by a Brood King.

3 The Magus is the dark version of Adam Warlock.

4 The Magus is killed and brought back to life as a child.

Galactus

5 The giant cosmic being Galactus eats stars.

6 Galactus has a herald who searches for food for him.

7 Galactus is present at the birth of the universe.

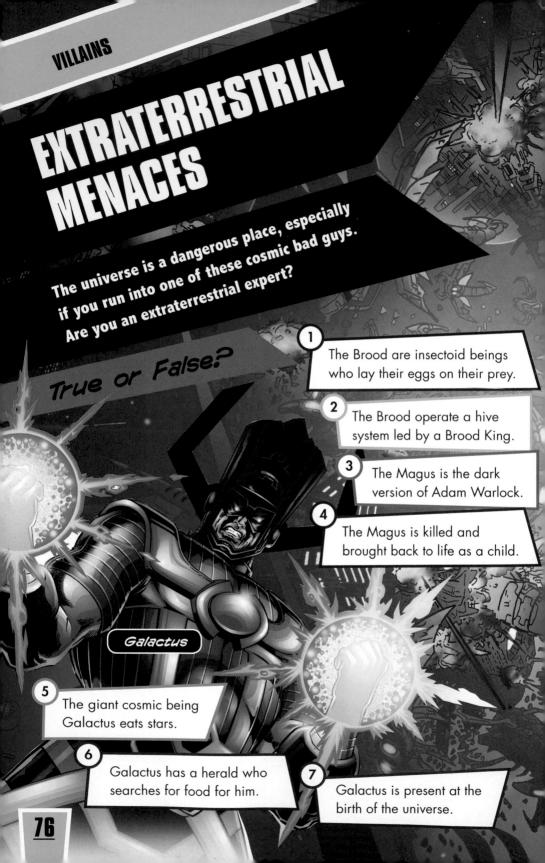

8 Ego is a living planet.

9 Ego's greatest enemy is Magus.

10 Ronan the Accuser is a Shi'ar.

11 As an Accuser, Ronan wields the Universal Weapon.

12 Ronan is married to a Skrull princess.

13 Mojo has named his homeworld after himself.

14 Mojo has created toddler versions of the Avengers and X-Men.

15 Annihilus is ruler of a dimension known as the Positive Zone.

16 Annihilus carries the powerful Cosmic Control Rod.

17 The evil Phalanx have bodies that are both organic and machine-based.

18 The cosmic Phoenix Force was once secretly an X-Man.

19 Skrulls are known for their flying abilities.

20 Skrulls have blue skin.

21 The immensely powerful Beyonder creates Battleworld so he can watch Earth's heroes fight.

ANSWERS

1 True – These unfortunates then become part Brood.

2 False – The hives are led by Brood Queens.

3 True – The opposite of Warlock's "perfect" being.

4 True – But he is soon plotting to destroy the universe again.

5 False – Galactus consumes the life energy of planets.

6 True – Silver Surfer is a former herald of Galactus.

7 True – He pilots a spacecraft from the preceding universe.

8 True – He is created when the consciousness of a scientist is merged with his homeworld.

9 False – Ego's nemesis is Galactus, who has tried to eat him in the past.

10 False – He is from the Kree Empire.

11 True – Only Accusers are able to use this mighty weapon.

12 False – He was married to the Inhuman Crystal.

13 True – He rules Mojoworld with an iron fist – and reality TV.

14 True – He hoped that they would bring in big ratings on his TV channels.

15 False – It is the Negative Zone.

16 True – This artefact gives him various powers and prolongs his life.

17 True – They feed on the energies of the people they conquer.

18 True – It took the place of Jean Grey, whom it had a connection with.

19 False – They are shape-shifters.

20 False – They are green in their usual form.

21 True – The Beyonder is the instigator of the first Secret Wars.

7 THINGS YOU NEED TO KNOW ABOUT...

Red Skull

5 He has a daughter named Sinthea – Sin for short.

6 Red Skull's regular henchman is the super-strong assassin Crossbones.

7 Red Skull has no super-powers of his own, so he is always in pursuit of powerful artefacts such as the Cosmic Cube.

GANGSTERS, THIEVES AND ASSASSINS

The underworld is full of shady characters making their living through organised crime and other illegal activities. How much do you know about these mobsters and mercenaries?

1

What is the real name of the ruthless crime boss known as the Kingpin?

a. Tilson Whisk
b. Bilson Brisk
c. Wilson Fisk
d. Samson Risk

2

True or false? Kingpin is so overweight that he has to use henchmen to do his dirty work.

3

Which Avenger is corrupt businessman Justin Hammer's main enemy?

a. Iron Man
b. Captain America
c. Black Widow
d. Vision

Genius Question

Which Avenger was a trained Hydra assassin before becoming a Super Hero?

4

Hitman Billy Russo is now known by which codename, after an attack by the Punisher?

a. Tombstone
b. Mister Negative
c. Count Nefaria
d. Jigsaw

5

What strange power does thief Felicia Hardy, a.k.a. Black Cat, possess?

a. Teleportation
b. Giving bad luck to opponents
c. Projecting an astral form of herself
d. Turning into a black cat

Bullseye

6 Mysterious but deadly assassin Bullseye once pretended to be which hero?
a. Spider-Man
c. Hawkeye
b. Iron Fist
d. Captain America

7 Which assassin is the child of the Greek Ambassador to the U.S.A.?
a. Elektra
b. Bullseye
c. Daken
d. Gamora

8 What is the codename of assassin Brock Rumlow?
a. Crossbones
c. Taskmaster
b. Hammerhead
d. Diamondback

9 Who is the father of organised crime queen Madame Masque?
a. Punisher
b. Kingpin
c. Mister Negative
d. Count Nefaria

10 Crime boss Hammerhead has a skull made from which material?
a. Vibranium
c. Uru
b. Adamantium
d. Gold

11 Which gangster has shaped all his teeth into sharp points?
a. Tombstone
c. Diamondback
b. Kingpin
d. The Big Man

12 Which crime boss transforms between human and Darkforce powers?
a. Count Nefaria
b. The Hood
c. Mister Negative
d. Silvermane

13 Which petty criminal gained super-powers by stealing a demon's cloak and boots?
a. Black Cat
c. Tombstone
b. The Hood
d. The Rose

14 Which gangster is forced to become a cyborg following an attack by Cloak and Dagger?
a. Diamondback
b. The Fixer
c. Silvermane
d. Boss Morgan

15 True or false? The mercenary Taskmaster can imitate any fighting style he sees.

ANSWERS

1c 2 False – Kingpin's bulk is almost pure muscle and he is a formidable fighter.
3a 4d 5b 6c 7a 8a 9d 10b 11a 12c 13b 14c 15 True – This ability
is called "photographic reflexes". **Genius Question** Spider-Woman

2.92m

Potential height of a human possessed by the curse of the Wendigo (9ft 7in).

152m

Height of a Humanoid robot weapon built by genius Super Villain and Hulk enemy the Leader (500ft).

WOW!

384,400km

The distance Red Hulk can cover in a single bound (238,835 miles). He once jumped all the way to Earth from the Moon!

Hulk vs Abomination

175

Weight in tonnes that Tony Stark can lift in his Hulkbuster armour, designed specifically to take down Hulk if he gets out of control.

OOPS!

139,000

The number of workers needed to repair New York City after Hulk and his allies go on the rampage during his war against the Illuminati.

NUMBER CRUNCH

Fittingly, the Incredible Hulk has faced some incredible foes in his time. Check out the stats on some of the biggest, baddest beings to call themselves enemies of the Hulk.

538°C

Heat that the gamma-powered Rhino can withstand in his armour (1,000°F).

2

Number of pieces Wolverine is torn into by Hulk during a fight between the Ultimate versions of the two on Earth-1610.

100,000+

Volts of electrical charge electromagnetic monster Zzzax can use to incinerate anything that stands in its way.

445kg

Weight of Emil Blonsky after his gamma-fuelled transformation into the terrifying Abomination (980lb).

1

Number of times Hulk has lost in a clash against the Thing. At the time, Hulk is less powerful than usual in his Mr Fixit form, while Ben Grimm is stronger.

4

Members of the U-Foes, a team of villains who blame Bruce Banner for stopping them gaining even greater powers. They are Vector, Ironclad, Vapor and X-Ray.

BOOM!

1,000,000

Number of exploding suns that Sentry's power is equal to. Sentry is the only hero powerful enough to stop former ally Hulk when he is rampaging during World War Hulk.

MEAN MACHINES

Many evil geniuses have tried to build robots to help carry out their evil plans and get the better of powerful Super Heroes.

2 When the Super-Adaptoid copies multiple powers, what **COLOUR** does it turn?
- a. Red
- b. Blue
- c. Purple
- d. Green

1 Which organisation creates the **SUPER-ADAPTOID?**
- a. Stark Industries
- b. S.H.I.E.L.D.
- c. Hydra
- d. A.I.M.

3 What was the name of the robot **TEAM** started by the Super-Adaptoid?
- a. Heavy Metal
- b. Robots Against Humanity
- c. R.O.B.O.T.S.
- d. Mean Machines

4 **TRUE OR FALSE?** The robot TESS-One is created to combat rogue super-soldiers.

Genius Question
What is the alter ego of robotics expert Starr Saxon?

Ultron

The Awesome ANDROID decided to become good after an encounter with which hero?

a. Iron Man   c. Spider-Man
b. Thor   d. Hawkeye

 Where would an opponent need to strike the Awesome Android's **BODY** to shut it down?

a. Nose   c. Earlobe
b. Belly button   d. Armpit

 Which **ALIEN CIVILISATION** created the Sentry robots to spy on other planets?

a. Skrulls   c. Badoon
b. Kree   d. Brood

 What is the name for the giant robots created to destroy **MUTANTS**?

a. Mutant-Hunters
b. Traskbots
c. Sentinels
d. X-Destroyers

 These mutant-chasing robots are built by another **ROBOT**. What is its name?

a. Master Mold
b. Trask-Prime
c. Master Builder
d. Template

 TRUE OR FALSE?
Ultron brainwashes the Avengers' butler, Jarvis.

 Which Avenger creates the evil robot **ULTRON**?

a. Steve Rogers
b. Thor
c. Vision
d. Hank Pym

 In an alternate future, Ultron has taken over the world. What is his **REIGN OF TERROR** called?

a. The Ultronverse
b. Age of Ultron
c. Kingdom of Ultron
d. Planet Ultron

 Who is Ultron's intended **ROBOT BRIDE**, who leaves him to join the Avengers?

a. Ultronna   c. J.E.N.Y.
b. Mrs Ultron   d. Jocasta

 Which **VILLAIN** falsely claims to have built destructive robot **ULTIMO**?

a. Mandarin
b. Justin Hammer
c. Obadiah Stane
d. Baron Zemo

Sinister Six

TEAM-UP

When Spider-Man's foes realise that they can't beat the web-slinger on their own, they decide to team up!

Mysterio
A master of illusions, Mysterio wants to become a Super Villain and gain notoriety by defeating Spider-Man. Failing on his own, he joins the Sinister Six.

Electro
Max Dillon is struck by lightning and gains super-powers. He uses them to try and rob his way to an easy life, and becomes an enemy of Spider-Man.

Kraven the Hunter
Big-game hunter Kraven becomes obsessed with the idea of hunting and capturing Spider-Man.

Vulture

This airborne villain is one of Spider-Man's first foes. He is involved in the Sinister Six's first plot – to kidnap people who are important to Spider-Man.

Sandman

Flint Marko has the ability to transform his body into sand and assume any shape. This troubled villain is a member of many incarnations of the Sinister Six, but has also been an ally of Spider-Man.

Doctor Octopus

Radiation causes Doc Ock's mechanical tentacles to become fused to his body. He is the founder of the Sinister Six.

SPIDER-MAN'S FOES

There is a seemingly endless list of villains hoping to bring down the friendly neighbourhood Spider-Man. Do you know your Goblins from your Hobgoblins?

1 Whose face appears on the Spider-Slayer robots when they first go after the web-slinger?
a. Peter Parker's
b. Norman Osborn's
c. Mary Jane Watson's
d. J. Jonah Jameson's

2 One of Spider-Man's strongest recurring foes, Aleksei Sytsevich is better known as what?
a. Lion   b. Rhino   c. Elephant   d. Buffalo

3 True or false? The Green Goblin has no super-powers.

4 Which fellow villain is the half-brother of the Chameleon?
a. Kraven the Hunter   b. Mysterio   c. Electro   d. Hydro-Man

5 What is the real name of the villainous Scorpion?
a. Eddie Brock   b. Cletus Kasady   c. Mac Gargan   d. Max Dillon

6 Which of these people has never used the Hobgoblin identity?
a. Roderick Kingsley   b. Ned Leeds   c. Phil Urich   d. Norman Osborn

7 Dr Curt Connors is a friend of Peter Parker, but who is his savage alter ego?
a. Doctor Octopus   c. The Lizard
b. Green Goblin   d. The Jackal

8 True or false? Eddie Brock, a.k.a. Venom, used to work for a newspaper just like Peter Parker.

9 Eddie Brock shared a cell in jail with which other future Spidey villain?
a. Otto Octavius   b. Norman Osborn   c. Max Dillon   d. Cletus Kasady

10 And which terrifying villain would that cellmate become?
a. Scorpion   b. Carnage   c. Electro   d. Mysterio

11 Which of Spider-Man's enemies tries to marry Aunt May?

a. Green Goblin   b. Venom   c. Kraven the Hunter   d. Doctor Octopus

12 What is the name of the alternate Avengers team started by Norman Osborn?

a. Dark Avengers   c. Goblin Avengers
b. Osvengers   d. Deadly Avengers

Genius Question

When Norman Osborn pretends to be a Super Hero, what is his code name?

Green Goblin

13 What is the name of the reality-hopping villain who hunts all spider-powered beings?

a. Merlin   b. Mordor   c. Morlun   d. Morbid

14 As well as the Sinister Six, which other villain team-up has Doctor Octopus led?

a. Cabal   b. Masters of Evil   c. Hellfire Club   d. Circus of Crime

ANSWERS

1d 2b 3 False – Green Goblin uses the Goblin Formula to gain various powers. 4a
5c 6d 7c 8 True – Brock was a journalist before he bonded with the alien symbiote.
9d 10b 11d 12a 13c 14b **Genius Question** Iron Patriot

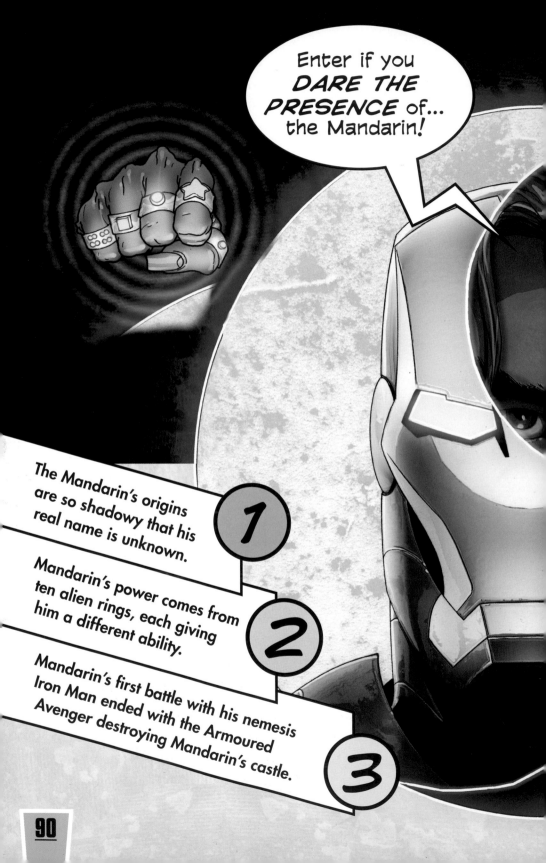

Enter if you **DARE THE PRESENCE** of... the Mandarin!

1 The Mandarin's origins are so shadowy that his real name is unknown.

2 Mandarin's power comes from ten alien rings, each giving him a different ability.

3 Mandarin's first battle with his nemesis Iron Man ended with the Armoured Avenger destroying Mandarin's castle.

5 THINGS YOU NEED TO KNOW ABOUT...

Mandarin

4 On one occasion, Mandarin is forced to allow Iron Man to use the power of his rings to defeat the dragon-like Fin Fang Foom and his alien comrades.

5 Mandarin's mastery of his inner chi power is so great that he is able to use it to survive years without food or water in a prison cell.

TEAM-UP

Cabal

When Norman Osborn gets control of S.H.I.E.L.D., he assembles his own secret super-team, the Cabal, to protect himself against payback from Earth's true heroes.

1

The Hood

This criminal, with powers granted by Dormammu, is charged with stopping the New Avengers from interfering with Osborn's Dark Avengers.

2

Norman Osborn

After killing the Skrull Queen during the Secret Invasion, Osborn is an unexpected hero. He is soon back to his scheming ways, and gathers the Cabal to help further his ambitions.

3

Loki

At this time Loki has taken the form of a woman. She tells Osborn she wants control of Asgard but, like the other Cabal members, she wastes no time in trying to bring him down.

4

Emma Frost

With her X-Men under threat, an alliance with Osborn at first seems like a good idea, but powerful telepath Emma Frost soon turns against the former Green Goblin.

5

Namor

Namor the Sub-Mariner is the only person to be a member of both the Cabal and its more heroic counterpart, the Illuminati. From the start he plots against Osborn.

6

Doctor Doom

The Latverian monarch uses Osborn to get back to his homeland, but never accepts his leadership. Osborn is left hoping that his Iron Patriot armour is enough to protect him if Doom turns against him.

WORLDS OF MARVEL

There's a multiverse out there filled with weird worlds and bizarre beings. There are also powers and weapons that stretch the limits of imagination, even right here on Earth!

EARTH

Earth is home to many Super Heroes and Villains, with connections stretching across the globe. Do you know your way around the heroic world?

1 Who is the ruler of the watery kingdom of Atlantis?
a. Black Panther
b. Hydro-Man
c. Namor
d. Mandarin

2 What is the name of the capital city of Atlantis?
a. Kamuu
b. Kamell
c. Canoo
d. Candoo

3 Which powerful team destroys Atlantis (although it is later rebuilt)?
a. Avengers
b. Squadron Supreme
c. Illuminati
d. Alpha Flight

4 Which race is not associated with the underground world of Subterranea?
a. Moloids
b. Lava Men
c. Deviants
d. Inhumans

5 Where on Earth is the Savage Land located?
a. Arctic
b. Antarctic
c. Bermuda Triangle
d. Amazon rainforest

6 True or false? Dinosaurs still exist in the Savage Land.

Genius Question
Which twin heroes are originally from the Republic of Transia?

Atlantis

7 What is the name of the hero who grew up in the Savage Land?

a. Bi-Zar
b. Ba-Zar
c. Ka-Zar
d. Ka-Boom

8 And what species of animal is his protector and companion Zabu?

a. Sabre-toothed tiger
b. Woolly mammoth
c. Tyrannosaurus
d. Pterodactyl

9 What is the capital city of Wakanda?

a. Cairo
b. Pretoria
c. Nairobi
d. Birnin Zana

10 True or false? Vibranium is only found in Wakanda.

11 What is the name of the country ruled by Doctor Doom?

a. Siberia
b. New Doom
c. Doomveria
d. Latveria

12 Which of these is the correct name for one of Wakanda's religious groups?

a. White Rabbit Cult
b. White Gorilla Cult
c. White Elephant Cult
d. White Meerkat Cult

13 What is the name of the ancestral homeland of the Inhumans?

a. Wakanda
b. Latveria
c. Attilan
d. Inhumania

14 Which of these maximum-security prisons is not found on Earth?

a. The Raft
b. The Cube
c. The Kyln
d. The Vault

15 Which hero owns a bar in the Asian island state of Madripoor?

a. Captain America
b. Wolverine
c. Iron Man
d. Star-Lord

ANSWERS

1c 2a 3b 4d 5b 6 True – The dinosaurs live alongside species from the Ice Age.
7c 8a 9d 10 False – Another type is found in the Savage Land. 11d 12b 13c
14c 15b **Genius Question** Scarlet Witch and Quicksilver

97

Being able to come to Avengers Mansion is... all kinds of **AMAZING.**
Hulkling

1 Avengers Mansion is located on Fifth Avenue in New York City.

2 The house was built in 1932 for the Stark family. Tony Stark allows the Avengers to use it as their headquarters.

3 The mansion is damaged and even destroyed on multiple occasions, but is always rebuilt.

4 As well as the main Avengers team, Avengers Mansion has also been used by the New Avengers and the Avengers Unity Division.

5 The above-ground section of Avengers Mansion contains living quarters and an aircraft hangar. Below ground are tactical and training rooms, a medical bay, generators and weapons storage.

10 THINGS YOU NEED TO KNOW ABOUT...

Avengers Mansion

6 Iron Man and Thor move the entire building 11m (35ft) further from the street for greater privacy.

7 Stark family butler Edwin Jarvis is a near-permanent fixture at Avengers Mansion. As well as regular duties like cooking and cleaning, Jarvis is often called upon to administer medical treatment or fix Quinjets.

8 On one occasion, the super-evil Red Skull and his daughter Sin secretly take up residence in the basement of Avengers Mansion.

9 After Tony Stark loses all his money, Avengers Mansion is turned into a theme hotel, although it soon falls back into Super Heroic hands again.

10 In the grounds of the mansion is a statue honouring the founding members of the Avengers. When this is destroyed, it is replaced with a statue of a more recent team line-up.

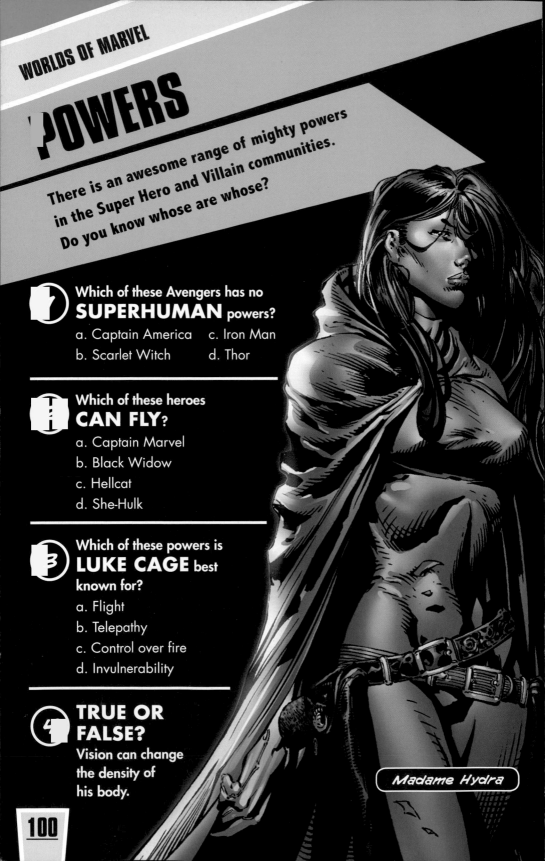

POWERS

There is an awesome range of mighty powers in the Super Hero and Villain communities. Do you know whose are whose?

1 Which of these Avengers has no **SUPERHUMAN** powers?

a. Captain America   c. Iron Man
b. Scarlet Witch   d. Thor

2 Which of these heroes **CAN FLY?**

a. Captain Marvel
b. Black Widow
c. Hellcat
d. She-Hulk

3 Which of these powers is **LUKE CAGE** best known for?

a. Flight
b. Telepathy
c. Control over fire
d. Invulnerability

4 **TRUE OR FALSE?**
Vision can change the density of his body.

Madame Hydra

Which of these heroes is not a
SIZE-CHANGER?
a. Ant-Man
b. Wasp
c. Goliath
d. Spider-Woman

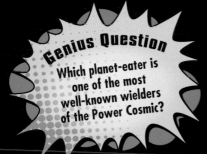
Genius Question
Which planet-eater is one of the most well-known wielders of the Power Cosmic?

 Which hero has **RADAR SENSE**, the ability to see all around himself despite being blind?
a. Iron Fist   c. Daredevil
b. Luke Cage   d. Spider-Man

 Which of the Runaways has the power of
SUPER-STRENGTH?
a. Karolina Dean
b. Nico Minoru
c. Gertrude Yorkes
d. Molly Hayes

 TRUE OR FALSE?
Evil mutant Apocalypse is very powerful but cannot fly.

 Which of these is an
ABILITY of Doctor Doom?
a. Hypnotism
b. Spell-casting
c. Genius-level intelligence
d. All of the above

 Magneto is the
MASTER of... what?
a. Mind control
b. Pie making
c. Magnetism
d. Time travel

 What is **VIPER**, a.k.a. Madame Hydra, an expert in?
a. Poison
b. Antique swords
c. Comic books
d. Cloning

 Which **IMMORTAL VILLAIN** uses his incredible powers mainly for amusing himself with games?
a. Thanos
b. Grandmaster
c. Galactus
d. Apocalypse

TRUE OR FALSE?
Carnage's strength is equal to Venom and Spider-Man's put together.

ANSWERS

1c 2a 3d **4** True – He can make himself either extremely dense, or intangible to allow objects to pass through him. **5d 6c 7d 8** False – Apocalypse can fly using the power of his mind, or by transforming his arms into wings. **9d 10c 11a 12b 13** True – He is a formidable – and truly nasty – opponent. **Genius Question** Galactus

2

Tridents of Neptune. One is owned by Neptune himself and the other by Namor the Sub-Mariner.

WOW!

7,620m

Height of the Godkiller armour, built by the Aspirants, a type of Celestial, to kill other Celestials (25,000ft).

0.76m

Diameter of Captain America's shield (2.5ft).

1

Times that Nico Minoru can use the Staff of One to cast any one spell. To get round the problem, she can cast the same spell in different languages.

WHOOSH!

180,367km

Distance Captain America is estimated to have thrown his shield in his lifetime (112,075 miles).

9.1m

Diameter of the area in which the wearer of the Cosmic Ring can alter reality (30ft).

65 million

The age of Mjolnir, Thor's hammer. It is thought that the explosion caused when Mjolnir was forged lead to the extinction of the dinosaurs on Midgard (Earth).

816°C

Temperature at which Wolverine's Adamantium claws would melt (1500°F).

NUMBER CRUNCH

The most amazing and the most dangerous weapons in the universe can be measured by their incredible statistics.

WEAPONS

1.8–7.6m

Length Doc Ock's tentacles can stretch (6–25ft).

1,448km.

Distance at which Doctor Octopus can telepathically control his tentacles (900 miles).

60

...and counting! The number of different Iron Man suits Tony Stark has built over the years.

2%

Percentage of full strength of the Infinity Gauntlet Thanos uses to sink the west coasts of the U.S.A. and Japan, and shatter the Bifrost Bridge. Imagine what he could do with the Gauntlet at full strength!

BUZZ!

30,000

Charge in volts delivered by Black Widow's "Widow's Bite" weapon.

WEAPONS

Heroes and villains often use cool weapons on their missions – although some are cooler than others!

1 True or false? Captain America's first shield is circular.

2 Which of these has never wielded Captain America's shield in battle?
a. Bucky Barnes   c. Scott Lang
b. Sam Wilson   d. Steve Rogers

3 True or false? Captain America's shield is indestructible.

4 What does Doctor Octopus use his tentacles for?
a. Fighting Spider-Man
b. Climbing walls
c. Rapid travel
d. All of the above

Genius Question
Which martial-arts expert and sometime assassin uses twin sai, three-pronged blades?

5 How many mechanical tentacles does Doctor Octopus usually wear?
a. One   c. Four
b. Two   d. Eight

6 True or false? Once fired, Spider-Man's web will dissolve after one hour.

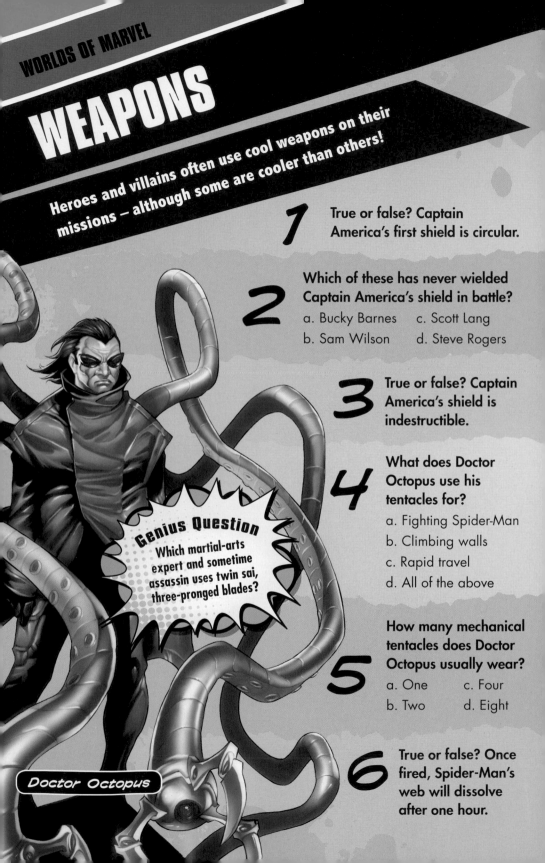

Doctor Octopus

7 Cap's shield is strengthened by Asgardian weapon-smiths with which material?

a. Platinum   b. Uru   c. Gold   d. Adamantium

8 Which Guardian of the Galaxy carries an Element Gun inherited from his royal father?

a. Groot   b. Star-Lord   c. Drax   d. Rocket Raccoon

9 What is the name of the container in which an archer like Hawkeye keeps their arrows?

a. Bag   b. Arrow sack   c. Hood   d. Quiver

10 Which of these does Spider-Man not use his web-shooters for?

a. Swinging between buildings   c. Making and firing nets
b. Trapping criminals   d. Catching insects

11 Where did Hawkeye get his amazing skills with a bow and arrow?

a. Time-travelling to meet Robin Hood
b. Working at a carnival
c. He was given the talent by a wizard
d. He was shot by an enchanted arrow

12 Where on his body does Spider-Man wear his web-shooters?

a. Wrists   b. Ankles   c. Head   d. Waist

13 Which of these is not a real trick arrow used by Hawkeye?

a. Jelly arrow   c. Tear gas arrow
b. Smoke bomb arrow   d. Net arrow

14 The Trapster invents a gun firing which substance?

a. Water   b. Glue   c. Cream   d. Acid

ANSWERS

1 False – Cap's first shield is triangular. **2**c **3** False – It is nearly indestructible, but has been shattered by extremely powerful beings like the Asgardian Serpent. **4**d **5**c **6** True – Otherwise New York City would be covered in it! **7**b **8**b **9**d **10**d **11**b **12**a **13**a **14**b **Genius Question** Elektra

105

SCIENCE AND TECH

For heroes and villains alike, when there are no mutations or natural-born super-powers, science and technology have to be used to get an advantage.

1 What is the Super-Soldier Serum combined with to turn puny Steve Rogers into a Super Hero?
a. Vibranium
c. Electricity
b. Vita Rays
d. Mashed bananas

2 How is the heavily armed Mark II Iron Man armour better known?
a. Big Gun Suit
c. War Machine Armour
b. Armed Armour
d. Battle Suit

3 What colour was Iron Man's very first armoured suit?
a. Blue
c. Yellow
b. Grey
d. Green

4 Which hero does not use Pym Particles to change their size?
a. Ant-Man
c. Wasp
b. Hulk
d. Giant-Man

5 Which of these super-strong characters did not get their powers from Gamma radiation?
a. Hulk
b. She-Hulk
c. Abomination
d. The Thing

6 The Connors formula, created to regenerate lost limbs, is also known as what?
a. Lizard Formula
c. Goblin Formula
b. Regrow 4000
d. Armbrosia

7 True or false? Adamantium is brought to Earth in a meteor.

8 Goblin Formula is created at which company?
a. Parker Industries
c. Oscorp
b. Allan Chemical
d. Stark Industries

9 Anti-Metal, which can turn nearby metals into liquid, is a form of which substance?

a. Adamantium   b. Vibranium   c. Uru   d. Gravitonium

10 The Infinity Formula, which keeps Nick Fury young, is created by which historical genius?

a. Leonardo da Vinci

b. Albert Einstein

c. Archimedes

d. Sir Isaac Newton

11 What are the "waldoes" found on Peter Parker's Iron Spider armour?

a. Mechanical arms

b. Cup-holders

c. Wings for flying

d. Holographic lenses

Genius Question

What is the name of the devices used by Spider-Man to track people and objects around N.Y.C.?

12 True or false? In a bid to be more human, Vision builds himself a robot family in a lab.

War Machine

13 What is the name of the prototype serum-turned-virus created by Dr Aldrich Killian and Dr Maya Hansen?

a. Ultimis   b. Extremis   c. Infinitis   d. Titanis

14 Which of these characters does not use a device for teleporting?

a. Nightcrawler   b. Cable   c. Guardians of the Galaxy   d. Deadpool

ANSWERS

1b 2c 3b 4b 5d 6a 7 False – The super-strong metal is created in a lab by Dr Myron Maclain.
8c 9b 10d 11a 12 True – He builds a wife named Virginia and two kids: Viv and Vin. 13b 14a
Genius Question Spider-tracers

5 THINGS YOU NEED TO KNOW ABOUT...

Asgard

1 Asgard is ruled by the All-Father Odin and his queen, Frigga. The heir to the throne is their son, Thor.

2 Asgard is one of the Nine Realms until Thor and Loki make peace with Heven, which becomes the tenth realm.

3 Inhabitants of Asgard can travel to other realms using the Bifrost, or Rainbow Bridge, guarded by the ever-watchful Heimdall.

4 After Asgard is destroyed, Tony Stark builds a new one named Asgardia, a technological marvel that hovers above Earth.

5 All Asgardians are much more powerful than humans from Earth, and they have extremely long lives.

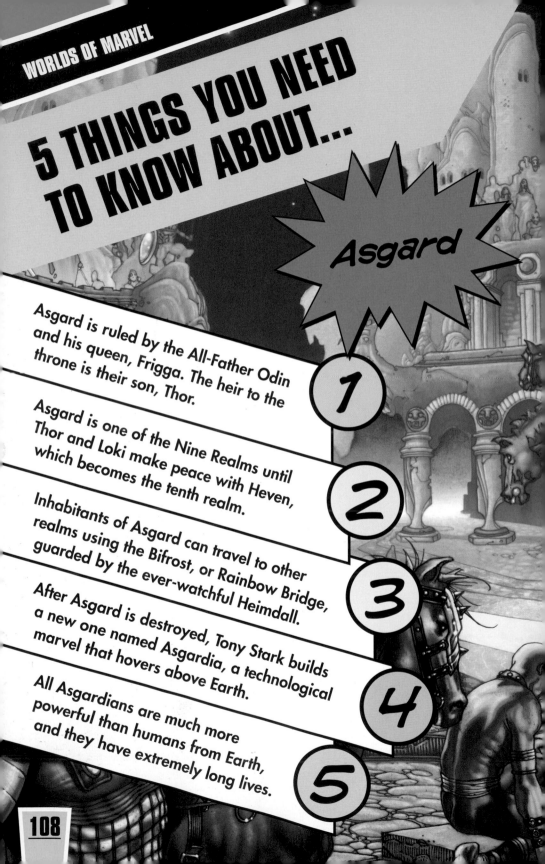

ALTER EGOS

Some heroes and villains keep their true identities a closely guarded secret, while others operate completely in the public eye. How many are known to you?

True or False?

1 Steve Rogers is Iron Man.

2 Natasha Romanoff is the Scarlet Witch.

3 Bruce Banner is the Incredible Hulk.

4 Kamala Khan is Captain Marvel.

5 Peter Quill is Spider-Man.

6 Jessica Jones was formerly known as Jewel.

7 Vision was once known as Victor Shade.

8 Danny Rand is Iron Fist.

9 Clint Barton is Falcon.

10 Happy Hogan is War Machine.

11 Jennifer Walters is She-Hulk.

12 Sam Wilson is the Winter Soldier.

13 Adam Brashear is Blue Marvel.

14 The villain Hobgoblin is really a fashion designer.

15 The Venom identity is used by Peter Parker's old classmate Flash Thompson.

Blue Marvel

16 Before being transformed into evil genius the Leader, Samuel Sterns is a respected scientist.

17 Victor Creed, a.k.a. Sabretooth, is the son of Wolverine.

18 Red Hulk is General Thaddeus "Thunderbolt" Ross.

19 Skill-duplicating villain Taskmaster's real name is Tony Masters.

20 Zebediah Killgrave is better known as the Magenta Man.

21 Kate Bishop is the second Hawkeye.

22 Adamantium-laced assassin Lady Deathstrike's real name is Laura Kinney.

ANSWERS

1 False – Steve is Captain America.
2 False – Natasha is Black Widow.
3 True – Although the two are very different!
4 False – Kamala is Ms Marvel.
5 False – Quill is Star-Lord.
6 True – She then gave up being a costumed hero.
7 True – He used this name when appearing to be human.

8 True – And a Hero for Hire!
9 False – Clint is Hawkeye.
10 False – It is James "Rhodey" Rhodes.
11 True – And the go-to attorney for Super Heroes!
12 False – It is Bucky Barnes.
13 True – He is one of Earth's most powerful superhumans.

14 True – Roderick Kingsley used the Hobgoblin persona to try and wipe out his rivals.
15 True – As Agent Venom, Flash turns the alien symbiote into something good.
16 False – Sterns is a janitor at a chemical research facility.
17 False – Wolverine has several children, but Creed is not one of them.

18 True – After years hunting the Hulk, Ross becomes a gamma-fuelled monster too!
19 True – He is a former S.H.I.E.L.D. agent gone bad.
20 False – Killgrave is the evil and manipulative Purple Man.
21 True – She shares the codename with Clint Barton.
22 False – It is Yuriko Oyama.

5 THINGS YOU NEED TO KNOW ABOUT...

Magical Artefacts

CLOAK OF LEVITATION
Used by Doctor Strange, the cloak enables him to fly and even helps fight his enemies.

1

EYE OF AGAMOTTO
This powerful object can only be used by someone pure of heart.

2

MJOLNIR
Thor's mighty hammer is made from Uru, a metal forged in the heart of a star.

3

STORMBREAKER
A magical war hammer wielded by Beta Ray Bill.

4

5

DESTROYER ARMOUR
Odin builds this enchanted armour to hold the power of all the gods.

Whosoever holds this *HAMMER*, if he be worthy, shall possess the power of Thor.

OTHERWORLDLY POWERS

The universe is a big place, and it contains all sorts of crazy cosmic weapons. Sadly, these often fall into the wrong hands.

Genius Question
Which alien villain creates the Cosmic Control Rod?

1 How many rings does Mandarin wear?
a. Two   b. Four   c. Eight   d. Ten

2 In which country does Mandarin find his rings?
a. China   b. Japan   c. Mongolia   d. Nepal

3 Which of these is the correct name for one of Mandarin's rings?
a. The Liar   b. Remaker   c. Nightbringer   d. All of the these

4 Which of Earth's villains is best known for his obsession with Cosmic Cubes?
a. Mandarin   b. Red Skull   c. Green Goblin   d. Doctor Octopus

5 True or false? A Cosmic Cube will eventually become a conscious being.

6 Which Avenger is turned into an agent of Hydra by a being evolved from a Cosmic Cube?
a. Iron Man   b. Hawkeye   c. Captain America   d. Scarlet Witch

7 Which race gets its powers from Terrigen crystals?
a. Inhumans   c. Shi'ar
b. Skrulls   d. Eternals

8 Where are Terrigen Crystals found?
a. In the Arctic
b. Under the city of Attilan
c. Inside asteroids
d. In Tony Stark's kitchen cabinets

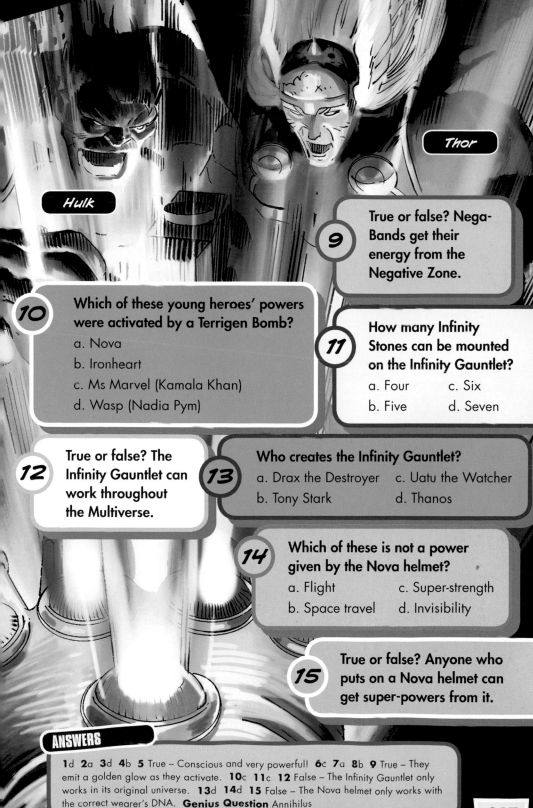

Hulk

Thor

9 True or false? Nega-Bands get their energy from the Negative Zone.

10 Which of these young heroes' powers were activated by a Terrigen Bomb?
a. Nova
b. Ironheart
c. Ms Marvel (Kamala Khan)
d. Wasp (Nadia Pym)

11 How many Infinity Stones can be mounted on the Infinity Gauntlet?
a. Four   c. Six
b. Five   d. Seven

12 True or false? The Infinity Gauntlet can work throughout the Multiverse.

13 Who creates the Infinity Gauntlet?
a. Drax the Destroyer   c. Uatu the Watcher
b. Tony Stark   d. Thanos

14 Which of these is not a power given by the Nova helmet?
a. Flight   c. Super-strength
b. Space travel   d. Invisibility

15 True or false? Anyone who puts on a Nova helmet can get super-powers from it.

ANSWERS

1d 2a 3d 4b 5 True – Conscious and very powerful! 6c 7a 8b 9 True – They emit a golden glow as they activate. 10c 11c 12 False – The Infinity Gauntlet only works in its original universe. 13d 14d 15 False – The Nova helmet only works with the correct wearer's DNA. **Genius Question** Annihilus

115

5 THINGS YOU NEED TO KNOW ABOUT...

Vehicles

SILVER SURFER'S BOARD
Arguably the universe's coolest vehicle, Silver Surfer's board is mind-linked to its owner and is virtually indestructible.

4

GHOST RIDER'S MOTORCYCLE
Nearly all those who use the Ghost Rider identity have ridden a motorcycle made from black magic and surrounded by flames.

5

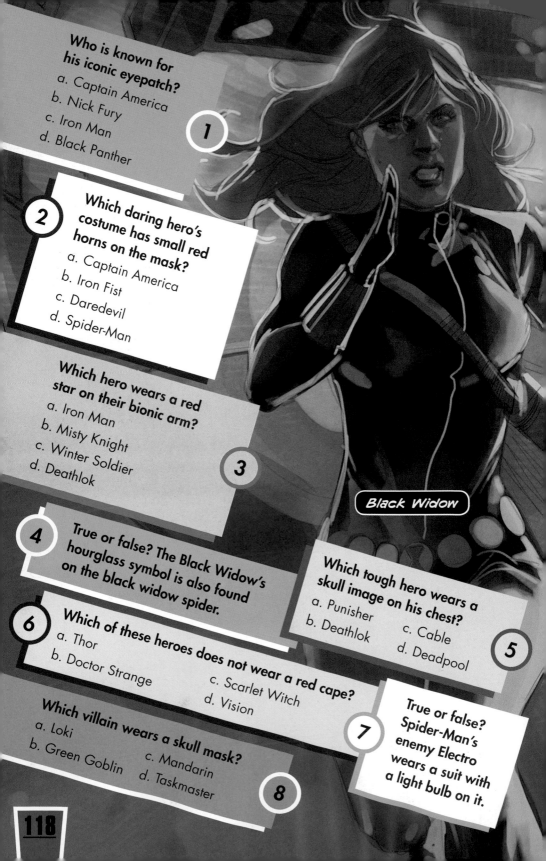

Who is known for his iconic eyepatch?
a. Captain America
b. Nick Fury
c. Iron Man
d. Black Panther

1

2

Which daring hero's costume has small red horns on the mask?
a. Captain America
b. Iron Fist
c. Daredevil
d. Spider-Man

Which hero wears a red star on their bionic arm?
a. Iron Man
b. Misty Knight
c. Winter Soldier
d. Deathlok

3

Black Widow

4 True or false? The Black Widow's hourglass symbol is also found on the black widow spider.

Which tough hero wears a skull image on his chest?
a. Punisher
b. Deathlok
c. Cable
d. Deadpool

5

6 Which of these heroes does not wear a red cape?
a. Thor
b. Doctor Strange
c. Scarlet Witch
d. Vision

Which villain wears a skull mask?
a. Loki
b. Green Goblin
c. Mandarin
d. Taskmaster

7 True or false? Spider-Man's enemy Electro wears a suit with a light bulb on it.

8

COSTUMES

No hero or villain is complete without an eye-catching costume. Do you know which suit belongs to which character?

9 Which of these Avengers traditionally wears a winged helmet?
a. Iron Man
b. Black Widow
c. Scarlet Witch
d. Thor

10 What symbol appears on the chest of Captain Marvel's costume?
a. Lightning flash
b. Star
c. The letter M
d. A phoenix

Genius Question

Which hero wears a high-tech suit containing Vibranium?

11 Who claims his suit is red so the bad guys can't see him bleed?
a. Iron Man
b. Deadpool
c. Ant-Man
d. Spider-Man

12 Which villain wears a vest made out of a lion's head, complete with mane?
a. Mysterio
b. Carnage
c. Kraven the Hunter
d. Crossbones

13 Which villain wears cloak and boots granting the power of the dread Dormammu?
a. The Hood
b. Baron Mordo
c. Mister Sinister
d. Enchantress

14 Which villain wears a battle suit with a whip-tail that delivers electrical blasts?
a. Doctor Octopus
b. Vulture
c. Scorpion
d. Lizard

ANSWERS

1b 2c 3c 4 False – She is named after a top-secret Russian training program, not the spider. 5a 6d 7 False – Electro's suit features gold lightning flashes. 8d 9d 10b 11b 12c 13a 14c **Genius Question** Black Panther

5 THINGS YOU NEED TO KNOW ABOUT...

Spider-Man Clones

1 Insane biochemist Miles Warren, a.k.a. the Jackal, creates clones of Spider-Man to get revenge on the web-slinger for the death of his student Gwen Stacy.

2 The Jackal creates many clones using Peter Parker's DNA, including Ben Reilly and Kaine.

3 For a time, Peter Parker clone Ben Reilly believes himself to be the real Spider-Man, but when he learns the truth he becomes the Scarlet Spider.

4 Kaine, the first clone of Peter Parker, is mentally unstable but capable of heroic deeds.

5 A six-armed duplicate of Spider-Man is created by Magus during the Infinity War. This monstrous being is even stronger than the original Spidey!

PLANETS

The universe is a big place, full of strange and wonderful worlds. Do you know which would be fun to visit — and which would be best avoided?

1 Which Super Hero was once the **RULER** of the planet Sakaar?

a. Captain Marvel   c. Thor
b. Star-Lord   d. Hulk

2 What is the main entertainment for the population of **SAKAAR**?

a. Blockbuster movies
b. Video games
c. Gladiator battles
d. Ballet shows

3 Which planet does Thanos' home **TITAN** orbit?

a. Saturn   c. Earth
b. Jupiter   d. Mars

4 **TRUE OR FALSE?**
Thanos is the last survivor of Titan.

5 Who builds the **ORIGINAL** "patchwork" planet of Battleworld?

a. The Beyonder   c. Tony Stark
b. Molecule Man   d. Thanos

6 The **SECOND BATTLEWORLD** is ruled by Doctor Doom, but who is his right-hand man and "Sheriff"?

a. Captain America
b. Doctor Strange
c. Spider-Man
d. Black Panther

7 Hala is the homeworld of which **ALIEN** empire?

a. Skrulls   c. Kree
b. Badoon   d. Brood

8 **TRUE OR FALSE?**
The vast space station Knowhere is built inside a giant head.

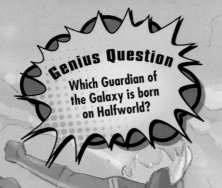

Genius Question

Which Guardian of the Galaxy is born on Halfworld?

11 The planet Counter-Earth is created by which unstable **GENIUS**?

a. Norman Osborn

b. Otto Octavius

c. The High Evolutionary

d. The Mad Thinker

12 The planet **XANDAR** is the birthplace of which intergalactic force?

a. Black Order

b. Nova Corps

c. Guardians of the Galaxy

d. Intergalactic Council

13 **TRUE OR FALSE?** The Worldmind is a space station orbiting Xandar.

9 The finest **MINDS OF HALA** are joined in an A.I. known as what?

a. Giant Brain

b. Mind Meld

c. Intellector

d. Supreme Intelligence

14 What is the name of the **CASINO PLANET** where Wolverine won money to fund his mutant school?

a. Vega   c. Win

b. Dolla   d. Sin

10 What is the name of the **SHI'AR** homeworld?

a. Chandilar

b. Candelabra

c. Kara'Vann

d. Shi'earth

15 Which alien originates from the planet **KLYNTAR**?

a. The Venom symbiote

b. Ronan the Accuser

c. Corvus Glaive

d. Ebony Maw

ANSWERS

1d 2c 3a 4 False – Although he did destroy almost all his fellow Titanians, some survived. 5a 6b 7c 8 True – It is the head of an ancient Celestial. 9d 10a 11c 12b 13 False – It is a supercomputer containing data on all Xandarians, past and present. 14d 15a **Genius Question** Rocket Raccoon

5 THINGS YOU NEED TO KNOW ABOUT...

Spider-Ham

1 Peter Porker lives on Earth-8311 – a reality populated by talking animals.

2 He is born a spider, but becomes a spider-powered pig after being bitten by May Porker, an irradiated pig.

3 Peter Porker is married to Mary Jane Waterbuffalo.

4 Spider-Ham is a member of the Warriors of the Great Web, along with many other spider-powered heroes from different realities.

5 Spider-Ham's enemies include Ducktor Doom, the Bull-Frog, Buzzard, Hogzilla and the King-Pig.

STRANGE DIMENSIONS

The universe is part of the Multiverse, where many strange realities play out, and many bizarre and wonderful heroes live.

1

Which designation is given to the Prime Earth?
a. Earth-1
b. Earth-101
c. Earth-616
d. Earth-1610

3

True or false? Gwen Stacy, the Spider-Woman of Earth-65 is in a band.

2

Which alternate 'Ultimate' universe is the original home of Spider-Man Miles Morales?
a. Earth-1
b. Earth-101
c. Earth-616
d. Earth-1610

5

Who is the ruler of the Dream Dimension?
a. Nightmare
b. Doctor Strange
c. The Dreamer
d. Sandman

4

Which of these is not an animal-themed Super Hero of Earth-8311?
a. Black Widow
b. Captain Americat
c. Iron Mouse
d. Deerdevil

6

How would you get to the Microverse?
a. On a tiny bus
b. On a super-fast spaceship
c. Using Pym Particles
d. On a Quinjet

7

In the very strange reality of Earth-9047, which villain takes on the mantle of Santa Claus?
a. Annihilus
b. Doctor Doom
c. Green Goblin
d. Thanos

126

8 What is the name of the hero who comes to Earth from Duckworld?
a. Brian the Duck
b. Henry the Duck
c. Chester the Duck
d. Howard the Duck

9 True or false? Inhabitants of the extradimensional realm Mojoworld are obsessed with Earth heroes who they watch on Mojoworld TV.

Genius Question
Who is queen of the Asgardian realm of Hel?

10 Who is the ruler of Olympus, a pocket dimension populated by gods?
a. Poseidon
b. Zeus
c. Hades
d. Hera

11 Which gloomy dimension is home to Prison 42?
a. Darkforce Dimension
b. Dark Dimension
c. The Negative Zone
d. The Prison Zone

12 Which hero can travel to the Dream Dimension using an astral form?
a. Doctor Strange
b. Captain Marvel
c. Vision
d. Hulk

13 True or false? The reality where Marvel Comics fans live does not exist in the Multiverse.

14 What is the nickname of May Parker, Peter Parker's daughter on Earth-982?
a. Spider-Baby
b. Webby
c. Mayflower
d. Mayday

15 What is Earth-001, the base of the Warriors of the Great Web, also known as?
a. Spider-World
b. Loomworld
c. Webland
d. The Nexus

16 Which of Spider-Man's family becomes "Golden Oldie", herald of Galactus, on Earth-8417?
a. His mother
b. His father
c. Uncle Ben
d. Aunt May

ANSWERS

1c 2d 3 True – The band is called the Mary Janes. 4a 5a 6c 7b 8d 9 True – To keep the citizens quiet, ruler Mojo tries to kidnap Earth heroes to make his own TV shows. 10b 11c 12a 13 False – Our world is designated Earth-1218, where Super Heroes are fictional. 14d 15b 16d **Genius Question** Hela

DK | Penguin
Random
House

Project Editor: Lisa Stock
Project Designer: Jessica Tapolcai
Pre-Production Producer: Marc Staples
Senior Producer: Jonathan Wakeham
Managing Editor: Sadie Smith
Managing Art Editor: Vicky Short
Art Director: Lisa Lanzarini
Publisher: Julie Ferris
Publishing Director: Simon Beecroft

First published in Great Britain in 2019
by Dorling Kindersley Limited
80 Strand, London WC2R 0RL
A Penguin Random House Company

19 20 21 22 23 10 9 8 7 6 5 4 3 2 1
001–311504–June/2019

MARVEL
marvel.com

©2019 MARVEL

A CIP catalogue record for this book is available from the
British Library

ISBN: 978-0-24135-758-3

Printed and bound in China

A WORLD OF IDEAS:
SEE ALL THERE IS TO KNOW
www.dk.com